The Elephant in the Room

Authors: Donald Brooks & Cynthia Prospers

ISBN-13: 978-0-5788-80297

DEDICATION

In Memory of Donald Leroy Brooks

August 31, 1953 -------- July 19, 2019

Beloved Husband, Father, Family Man and Humanitarian

A Few Moments with A King

Cynthia Prospers Brooks

I found my late husband, Donald Brooks, to be a great demonstrator of "loving your neighbor as yourself." I always enjoyed listening to his witty sayings. He would sometimes say, "A woman that can't learn from her man, really don't have a man." I believed that to be true from our relationship. His sayings and life experiences that he shared with me were mesmerizing. It amazed me how he took past tragedies of loss, abuse, drug addiction, and homelessness and turned them into triumphs. He made lemonade out of lemons.

One of the relationships treasures I learned from him was, finding out what people liked and providing it or some form of it for them. It was the little things he did that made people feel special. In an example, during his "Man's night out" with his friends, he would dance with ladies who did not have a date or with women whose partners could not dance. He was very respectful and enjoyed dancing. The women waited their turn to dance with him. A woman he had danced with years prior, approached him and thanked him for helping her friend who was dying from cancer feel special. He danced with her and gave her a rose. Donald had no clue of that woman's situation. He shared with me that he didn't know he was a part of helping to put a smile on her face.

I witnessed him arrange to have sweet tea made and brought to a former department head who enjoyed drinking sweet tea and which was not a menu item. On Valentine's Day before his death, he purchased two dozen roses and gave a rose to all the women on his job with whom he worked. He did not discriminate. He shared three stories with me, which included one married woman that cried tears of joys because it was her first time receiving a rose. Another woman who had not been kind to him looked at him with a piercing stare. He said to her that he was not dwelling on to whatever disagreement experienced between them. I asked if she took the rose and he said that she did. Afterward, she was more tolerable. Donald also shared that one woman complimented him saying; "You are a real O.G. (Original Gangster) *gentleman.*"

He never ceased to amaze me as I witnessed how he talked to people. He seemed to give them just what they needed. His thoughtfulness was respected and appreciated. He communicated individually and in group settings in ways that the hearer could understand and receive. I learned from him how to turn a negative situation into a positive one. I remember being upset because certain people were claiming to be related to him just to get special treatment and favor. I came home angry one day and told him that someone was using his name in vain. I was expecting him to get upset and address the person. He, on the other hand, paused and replied humbly, "I'm honored that someone thinks enough about me to use my name to get head of the line privileges." I must say that I was taken aback and learned a new lesson that day on loving your neighbor as you love yourself.

Don had to love himself through homelessness, drug addiction, being jailed, and an outcast as he made his return to society. During his darkest moments, he learned and remembered available resources that he would share and continue to share with others needing assistance. He became an asset to society and a notable change agent in Washington, DC, and surrounding areas.

I am thankful that I did not listen to people who told me to stay away from him because he was "bad news and a loudmouth." Donald Brooks "rubbed me the wrong way" when I first met him. I thought he was an arrogant loudmouth too. I felt his verbal delivery could have been more polished instead of brash. He did not mince his words and said whatever was on his mind. I took offense to his opinion of people, politics, religion, and life scenarios. Realizing that I was offended, I had to ask myself why I took offense in the first place. What was it inside of me that resembled what he said? I had to do a self-inventory. I realized that it was people-pleasing and not being true to myself and my beliefs. Since I learned that lesson from him, I decided not to judge him and get to know him better. I learned that he was a passionate man. Mr. Brooks was full of compassion, wisdom, experience, a great communicator, and a friend to humanity.

Getting to know my neighbor as myself led to me standing in my power even when I had to stand alone. It led to taking heart in what I believe. It led to loving myself and being myself unapologetically. It led to us getting married and having a beautiful ten-month and ten days of true love and wedded bliss until his untimely and unexpected death. We loved each other as if it were our last day on earth. We lived and loved on purpose. We loved each other freely and enjoyed ourselves.

Table of Contents

A Salute to My Mother

Doris Brooks

November 24, 1934 – November 14, 2018

Donald Brooks

I think about Gerald and Eddie Levert singing, "The Wind Beneath My Wings." It brought it back to Gladys Knight's version. I think about my mother because I still haven't gotten over her recent passing. I try to go about my everyday life taking care of my wife, supporting my sisters and brothers, and being there for my daughter.

I can't forget, and I'll never forget being under the wings of my mother, who accepted me back into her life, guided me, and is still guiding me. She has shown me the proper and correct way to treat a hard-working and respectable woman, which filters down to my wife, my sisters, and my daughter. This made me treat them with the respect that they deserve. I think about the lessons teachable moments she had for me, whether we were either just alone or sometimes in a group.

Through her eyes, the movement of her body, or her smile. As much as I try to emulate her in different ways, some ways could never be emulated because she had her unique style. As much as my sisters stipulate that they would like to be like her, it is impossible because her shoes were too big to be filled.

Thinking about my mother, I am truly honored to have found my way back into her life before she left this life. I was truly honored to feed her, talk to her, hold her and tell her my issues and problems before she transcended. I just hope that I can continue to be the big brother, the uncle, the nephew, the father, the husband, and the man she inspired, instructed, and informed me to be. That is all I could ever wish for until I transcend to where I'm supposed to be in this life or the next one if there is another one. This is not goodbye but goodnight.

Words are not enough, but as I have gotten older, I realize that she was bigger than life and had motivated so many people. People are still coming up to me saying, "Oh, I didn't know Doris was your mother, or I'm sorry for your loss. Doris has done so much for my family and me." They talk about how much they miss her, even when I have my solitary moments, I play the tape of her instructing me to do something or go somewhere to help somebody else. She wasn't bothered by those that didn't like her or had negative feelings or thoughts.

She would just say, "Just do it." She was the Nike before Nike was ever in this generation or before Nike had taken the slogan of my mother and made it universal, "just do it," because that's who my mother was, "just doing it." I ride around this city and look at the Convention Center, the Verizon Center, and the properties going up in the Washington (DC) area. I realize how much influence she had on a lot of things. I watch how sisters, especially my sisters, are still grieving and don't even know it because she was the only one that could keep them in some type of focus. She kept them focused on what they need to do, should do, and have to do because they are all over the place mentally and physically. They don't even realize the influence my mother had over them to keep them guided. I see the disarray of where my family is now because they haven't come to grips, even today with my mother's departure.

Hopefully, we can find that focus again because she made us focus. She was like the laser beam in our lives. Hopefully, I haven't strayed too far because I know why things are out of focus. She helped me to realize what my purpose is and having her in my life has made me a better person, and a better man. Thank you.

Legacy to My Children

To my children/stepchildren, Louis, LaTina, Q. Jordan, Steven Malik and Da'Twan, Tahj, Kenny, my late husband's children, and my spiritual children. The legacy that I leave to you is to ensure that whenever you leave a place, leave it better off than when you arrived. Make something from nothing!

 Fear is false evidence appearing real. The answer is on the other side of fear. That is the secret. Fear is a façade. It is like a mirage. Get past it. Walk through it. Go over it. Go around it. Go under it. Get to the other side of fear.

Your life depends upon your actions. How else will people know that you have been here? Will your movie last forever? What about your legacy? What will you pass to your children? Where will the world see your name of being a value creator? Martin Luther King, Jr., Abraham Lincoln, Harriet Tubman, Dr. Myles Munroe, Sr. and Donald Brooks live beyond the grave. What will you add to this earth and universe? What value will you create? How will you make it better? When will you do your part? Understand that you can be, do and have what you desire. Everything you need is already inside of you. You were born rich! Speak it, receive it as done. You are what you think you are. You are what you say you are.

Study to show yourself approved and put some action behind it. Don't get philosophically obese by not doing anything with your purpose. You have to (take action) exercise what you learn. What you put in you must be exercised out of you. Exercise with the appropriate diet makes you physically fit and healthy. You will also feel good about yourself. You have to physically do something towards obtaining your purpose, goals, and dreams. As your mother, etc., you know and remember that I have taken things that were not considered valuable and created art and masterpieces out of them.

With the help of God, I've taken my dreams and made them a tangible reality. There are things I may not finish in this lifetime. However, my successors, who I have passed my vision to, will run with it across the finish line. I am currently carrying out what my late mother passed on to me. I have completed and am still completing things she wanted to see accomplished. On the other hand, I was anointed to be her successor through similar visions instilled in me.

Receive the gift of my legacy of being a value creator of leaving a place better off than when I arrived. If you look at my military history, I was the first military administrative and African American female in the history of Electronic Attack Squadron 209 to make Chief Petty Officer as a Full-Time Support personnel.

I created a Reserve Transition Assistance Program Brief for Reservists to aid them in retirement from the US Naval Reserve. It is still being utilized today. I began creating it in 1999 as a result of the request of the dire need. I transitioned to the Fleet Reserves from the US Navy in 2007. My official thirty-year retirement is July 31, 2017. Sailors who worked for me advanced and received some form of recognition. I added value and led by example.

I ask you again. What will you do? How will you add value? What is your purpose here? Identify your purpose. It's something you do every day. What is that thing you do that you enjoy doing and will do for free? Whatever that is, do it. Let your life speak beyond the grave. I love you, children.

I'm also known as a bully slayer. I fought bullies for friends. I didn't like seeing injustices, and I stood up and fought against them. I soon learned from skilled Naval Officers and Chief Petty Officer's how to fight peaceably with a pen and paper using my words. I can't be redundant enough in asking… "What will you do my children? Louis what are you doing? LaTina what are you doing? Q. Jordan what are you doing? Steven Malik and Da'Twan, what are you doing? Are you standing up and taking action? My children, this is a call to response. Why are you here? Identify your "why". You are here. You are leaders. You were once followers. "The greatest tragedy in life is not death, but it's the life that has not fulfilled its purpose. (Dr. Myles Munroe, Sr.)."

Children find your purpose. Don't make the graveyard rich with your gift(s) that you never shared. If you die without fulfilling your purpose, then you would have failed yourself, others, and your purpose for being here. We are only here for a prescribed time, and the time is not that long.

It seems that it was only yesterday that I got the news that I was going to be a mother. It seems like it was only yesterday when I held you Louis, LaTina and Q. Jordan in my arms and smelled your baby breaths. It is a pleasure being your mother and role model. Thank you for being my teacher.

I saw family members and friends on their deathbed, wishing for more time and could not get it. They died without finishing what they wanted to do. In the year 2013 my mother, your grandmother, Mattie Sylvia (Scott) Farmer transitioned and in 2019, my late husband Donald Brooks passed-away too, I saw the urgency of my purpose here on earth, magnified and lifted up. It was the recommission for me to go, do, and carry out my purpose. Their transition helped fuel me not to waste time with people who are not helping me to grow and get to my destination.

I want to share a word of wisdom. Avoid the trap of dream killers. They are the victims who want you to feel sorry for them, or people wanting you to remain in a victimized state. Don't go there. "If you are there, get out of it." Don't take on the "damsel in distress" mentality. Use it as a steppingstone to step up and out. You are above that. Yes, you went through those painful experiences and challenges. However, you went through it to minister to someone else to help them up and out (if they want help and will take the necessary steps towards freedom). Kings and Queens, you got this! You are value creators with a purpose! I thank God for you, and I love you!

Introduction

"The Elephant in the Room" is based on life challenges (opportunities) that, if addressed, may encourage our greater selves. How often do you ignore the obvious that is staring at you in the face? It's practically in the room where you are. There are things and/or events that we have experienced and were told to be quiet about. We have been conditioned by society on how to act.

You know some of the clichés. Children should be seen and not heard. Sticks and stones may break your bones, but words will never hurt me. A lady or gentleman is to act this way. Being in this or that group means that you have arrived and are a part of the status quo. You have to live right and die to get your pie in the sky. It's better to be tried by twelve than to be carried by six. Turn the other cheek. Pretend like you don't see them, and they will go away.

Imagine that you are watching television and a large elephant is in the same room with you. Its size, smell, trunk, poop droppings, and noises would be hard to ignore *at first*. I say *"at first"* because it would be annoying. However, in society, we have been taught how to ignore the obvious to the point of oblivion. We may have even shifted the responsibility or blame on others.

Don and I believe that change must first begin with the individual self (me, you). We must acknowledge the obstacle/problem and take the necessary steps to get to the other side of the obstacle/problem. We found it helpful to look at ourselves to see where we may have been a contributing factor. We decided to make the necessary changes in ourselves through spiritual, personal, professional, and emotional development. As long as people are on this earth, growth is a must. I've always found this particular phrase to be true, "If we are not growing, then we are dying." I'm not sure of its actual origination as I heard many people and groups use the previous phrase.

Every human being has an earthly purpose to fulfill. I believe that we are all here on earth in this appointed space of time to fulfill our purpose. We are the expression of God personified. We are all "born rich" with different personalities, talents, and gifts. They are to be used to add increase and value in this earthly realm.

In the following topics, Don and I share our collaborative and individual points of view. The *"His Story"* headings are the words of the late Donald Brooks that were recorded and written prior to his untimely passing. The *"Her Story"* headings are the words of Cynthia Prospers (Brooks).

The Need to be Safe

As human beings, we have certain needs that are non-negotiable. One of the needs is safety. "Safety needs in Maslow's hierarchy refer to the need for security and protection. When we have our physiological needs for food and water met, our safety needs dominate our behavior. These needs have to do with our natural desire for a predictable, orderly world that is somewhat within our control. Safety needs in today's world can manifest themselves as job security, savings accounts, insurance policies, financial security, and health and well-being" (http://study.com/academy/lesson/maslows-safety-needs-examples-definition-quiz.html).

It's interesting how I can remember a lot of life events in my primary years of life. One of my greatest memories is feeling "little girl safe" with my Daddy. I believe it's a feeling that is a natural part of the female make-up. Certain memorable events are prior to the age of two. I remember being "the essence" of me, Cynthia, as Daddy held me close to his heart. In his arms as a baby, I felt safe. He would say, "Hey Baby." His voice was very distinctive. I could pick him out of a crowd blindfolded. Daddy's voice has always been a source of assurance and comfort for me. I knew whenever I spoke to or saw him, everything was alright. You see, daddy was in the Army and would go away frequently and be gone long lengths of time. I was always looking with a longing for him. I used to put my toddler feet in his slippers because they made me feel close to him. Daddy was always happy to see us, my brother and I, and we him. I would always look to see if daddy was still home because I didn't know when he would be gone again.

Another form of safety for me was my pacifier. Mommy had a couple of pacifiers around the house for me. I remember suckling them for security. One day, I couldn't find my favorite pacifier. I think my mother was trying to wean me from it and threw it away. I was determined to find it. I searched high and low. I looked from my "two feet high" eye level to floor level. I sought and found it! I crawled under my bed and "struck gold." "That's right; I found my other pacifier," covered in dust. I wiped it off and suckled away contently. I conquered. Since I found my thinking apparatus (pacifier), I can do anything! I was unaware that I was implementing the "seek and find" principle. I knew that I was determined and had to find what I was looking for. I found it, and all was well in my world. That same "seek and find" determination rings true in me today.

I am always on some type of mission to complete. Life never ceases to amaze me. It's always exciting. My life continues to give way to enlightenment or that "aha" moment that causes the puzzle pieces to come together. I always looked for the way, the why, and the how. My curiosity and thirst for knowledge would sometimes lead to me getting scolded.

Because of my adventurous spirit, my parents would try to protect me from getting hurt. For some reason, the oven was fascinating to me. It was white, square, warm, and had a handle on it. What was its purpose? I had concluded that I would research the matter. I decided that I would begin my quest by touching the white square. To get a closer look, I carefully made my way over to the stove as it was referred to by my parents. As I began my slow and careful approach, from nowhere, my mother emerged. "No, no." "Don't touch that." "It's hot," Mommy said in her extremely concerned voice. I could not understand why she would get in the way of my progress. I just wanted to see what it would do. I assured myself that I would touch and become better familiar with that oven—my repeated attempts to make it to the stove while my mother wasn't looking, failed. I kept encountering setbacks. It was as if she had eyes in the back of her head or something. "Here she was, stopping me again." Daddy sternly said to her, "leave her alone and let her touch it." Once she touches it, she'll never touch it again." My mother reluctantly allowed me to proceed. This time, when I headed towards the oven, mommy didn't stop me. I felt invincible. Wow, I'm finally getting the opportunity to embark on a new experience! This is my exciting moment of truth! I stretched out my hand to touch the big square, white box. It emitted a warm presence. I touched it, and to my surprise, "it hurt." "It really hurt." "It burned me." This wasn't the results I was expecting. Is that what Mommy meant by saying, "it's hot?" I screamed in pain, and I got truly angry because Daddy and Mommy let me get hurt. "What were they thinking?" I cried, knowing that Daddy would come to my rescue. I waited, and he didn't come. Instead, Daddy looked at me and said, "I bet you won't touch that stove anymore." Well, he was right. I didn't touch *that* stove anymore. That event was a painful teachable moment. I felt betrayed by my big protector. That experience left an indelible mental and emotional mark on me. I still remember the sternness in my father's voice. Today, when I hear the sternness of my father's voice, I listen with my heart and consider the matter.

If a father is in his daughters' life, he is the first male image that she sees. She takes her cues from her father in how to handle certain situations.

Enlightening Moment: The lesson of the stove has increased my awareness of respect. Everything cannot be approached or applied in the same manner. There are laws set in place that will provide protection if they are adhered to. It wasn't that I couldn't touch the stove so-to-speak. I just couldn't touch it at that time. I was too young and didn't know the rules. I needed the proper instructions/guidance and protective handling tools to assist me. It would have also helped me to be taller and more mature (older). There are people in our lives who know where dangers await. They "have been there or done that." They may even know others who have experienced certain situations. Their sharing can serve not only as a wealth of information; it can also serve as a life preserver. It's up to each person if they choose to heed sage advice or reap the rewards of their actions.

What life giving lesson have you experienced? (Example: I burned my hand on a hot stove...)

____

____

____

____

____

____

____

What was your enlightening moment? (Example: I wasn't prepared to touch the hot stove…)

____

____

____

____

____

____

____

How can you apply what you have learned to your current experience today?
(Example: I must prepare myself to receive the desired outcome in my
business…)

____

____

____

____

____

____

____

What is a note of gratitude that you can give that brought you to this point in
your life? (I am thankful that I listen with my heart, consider the matter and
ask questions…)

____

____

____

____

____

The Perfect Family/Union

"People who die without achieving their full potential rob their generation of their latent ability." Dr. Myles Munroe, Sr.

How often do we enter relationships, families, join churches, fraternities, clubs, organizations or work in jobs/careers, etc., believing those entities will complete us?

We may say, "When I get married; If I become an Omega, Delta, Mason, Eastern Star…; If I join a certain church/ministry/denomination…; If I join the military; If I attend a particular college/university; If I work for this company; If I buy these shoes; When I get my house; When my ship comes in; When I get myself together, etc." Do any of these statements sound familiar to you? Maybe you even recited some of them. On another spectrum, you may have heard these clichés, "every family has that one family member who is a drunk, religious fanatic, narcissist (drama queen/king), fighter, black sheep, goody two shoes, etc."

Have you ever considered why our family members are the way they are? Could it be family secrets that are hidden and were never addressed? Secrets may have been hidden to avoid family and public shame. They may have been told or threatened not to tell anybody but God. They may have been told to take those secrets to their grave, and some did. Maybe you have heard,

"trouble don't last always but heaven is forever." Maybe you were told you must "work hard and die to get your pie in the sky." Are you waiting to get your "mansion in the sky and walk those streets paved with gold?" In the meanwhile, the family member who has suffered an injustice is walking through a living hell.

They are crying out for help and justice, and freedom. Their way of dealing with their hell may be acting out in some form of action, medication, drug, etc. to get temporary relief from their secret. "Take one for the team or in the name of the family." "Pretend not to see the elephant in the room."

For healing to take place, the secrets need to be addressed and dealt with. Secrets have fostered the art of people-pleasing, which has been a taught and learned behavior that has embraced the lie that people-pleasing saves lives and leads to success, and the lack of people-pleasing leads to ruin and death. Fear is the root of failure. The fear of rejection, insecurity, religious reasoning, other people's opinion, etc., are some of the reasons why people fail to reach their goals and miss love or business opportunities.

Imagine going to college to become a lawyer when you really want to be a chef, teacher, musician, actress, etc. You may have been told that certain occupations are more financially secure than others. There are people who love us and believe that they know what is best for us.

However, what they believe, may not be what is best for us. We are accountable for our actions and receive the rewards for our actions. How will you answer the question, "Did you complete your assigned purpose/mission?" If your answer is not "yes," then you have failed. There are people who were on their deathbed and suddenly realized that they didn't complete their goals and dreams.

Let's look at starting a family. Starting a family may cause anguish for the new couple. Their families may be either for or against the new union. There may be concerns as to where they fit or will fit in with the new arrangement. Can they still get financial support? What about their inheritance? What does the new spouse want? What's in it for them? On-the-other-hand, what about the other family members (parents, siblings, cousins, etc.) and friends? "I refuse to call him dad." "I refuse to call her mom." "She's no sister-in-law of mine." If you are or have been the "go-to" person whom your family has come to depend on, there may be reluctance on having to share you. Some family members may fear that the intended spouse/fiancé will take away the valuable time/errand they would normally spend/do with or for them.

Couples must establish boundaries with their families. You may have to say, "look, this is my husband, wife, or partner. You may not like him or her, but this is who I chose to love, and I would appreciate respect from both sides." Affirm your love for your family members and let them know there is room for them.

Her Story

Growing up, my life wasn't what I thought it should be. I wanted my family to be complete with my parents and siblings. Instead of what I thought my happy family should look like, I felt that I got the short end of the stick. I was very young when my parents completed their marriage. I hated the Army for taking my daddy away from me for so long.

To protect myself, I built an emotional wall. To avoid rejection and its pain, I trained myself not to get my hopes up. I realized that my parents' relationship and purpose as husband and wife was completed. I learned and accepted that regardless of their marital status, they still loved me. I said to myself and others, "when I get married, I'm going to be married until death do us part." I was in for the long haul. There wasn't going to be any divorce. We would talk through our problems, raise our children in a loving three-bedroom home with a white picket fence and a porch. Our porch would have two rocking chairs as we retired to play with our grandchildren. It was the American dream. I had it all figured out. Love would be enough to conquer all. After two completed marriages, I learned that love only was not enough. Time and circumstances would prove that it takes knowledge and the ability to love, tolerate, partnership, and the willingness to improve are key ingredients in the success of any relationship. Of course, change begins within us as individuals.

Maybe my parents didn't know better. They did their best with the information that was passed down from the previous generations. There are some areas where I felt my parents could have done more nurturing. Those areas where I felt a lack, were the main areas where I ministered to my children. However, what if those areas were not needed by my children? I did the same things my parents did, which was doing my best with the information I received. Just as I love my children and want the best for them, so did my parents for me. I learned that my children were individuals and have different personalities. Some forms of correction did not apply to them.

I had to find what worked and what was most effective. Let me tell you, I failed forward sometimes and had to go back to the drawing board as well as seeking out professional help. It's also true that not every partner will be willing to change. Their unwillingness may lead to divorce or the end of the marriage so to speak. With that being said, the individual can still make changes within themselves for betterment and forward progress in their life. After all, we can't change people. They must be willing participants. In order to obtain healthy success, it is my true belief that being a willing participant is non-negotiable.

There was a time in life when I thought I had the meanest mother in the world. I felt like I was Cinderella having to shoulder most of the burden to take care of the house and assist in raising my younger siblings. I believed that I was held to a higher standard than my other siblings. I didn't think it was fair that I could not go to a lot of places with my friends. I could only go to school, church, home, and family member's homes. I began applying learned domestic abilities at the age of five. I became the caretaker of the house at age 13. Eighteen could not come soon enough for me to leave and live my own life. I decided to keep my eyes and head straight forward and not look back. I strongly affirmed that the only time I would grace my hometown or my mother's house with my presence would only be to visit. In my eyes at that time, Ma didn't seem to know or understand much. As a matter of fact, in my eyes, she was a bit old fashioned and sometimes hypocritical.

At the age of twenty, I became a mother and finished having my birth children at age twenty-four. As my children grew, I realized that Ma might have been onto something after all. She may have known what she was talking about on some things. By the time I birthed my second of three children, my mother had started treating me as an adult child. After the birth of my third child, we began swapping mom stories.

My youngest brother is a year older than my son. I guess you can say that we were almost having babies together. We began talking more and became friends. One of the greatest blessings for me was that I was able to address my childhood traumas and understand things from her point of view. We had come to a place of being able to share stories without fear of judgment. We were able to redeem the time.

His Story

The perfect family for me is two-fold. It can be my children or my wife. The perfect family is the most imperfect thing it's supposed to be. It's the both of us growing, making mistakes. It's the both of us growing and laughing at our mistakes. It's the both of us loving ourselves… constantly showing physical or emotional love to each other and strength. "I'm not killing her dream, and she's not killing mine."

We're working together to make sure that we're striving to reach the goal that we set for ourselves as a unit, and hopefully, a lot of her personal goals are being reached at the same time. Don't look for perfection, or else you will always fall short. That means you will always be unhappy. It's no such thing as a perfect family. It's only for being perfectly compatible and happy and loving. That's the only type of perfection we hope to get out of our union.

<u>Enlightening Moment:</u>

We must work on ourselves first and be the change we want to see. Sometimes we try to fix things that are beyond repair. We may try to open closed doors that should remain closed. We may even try to salvage a relationship that's just not going to work. When a person, organization, thing, situation and/or event served its purpose, the respective relationship begins to close.

Loyalty, prestige, advancement, benefits, and commitment, etc., are some of the wrong reasons to remain in an unhappy situation. Closed doors shouldn't be viewed as a "doomsday." Instead, see them as opportunities for new beginnings.

Your family members will still live their lives, and you must live yours. You may face obstacles (opportunities) from both sides of the family. Remember who chose love and why you married each other. Remember why you both said, "I love *me some* her, and I love *me some* him!" The couple must "draw the line in the sand" and set boundaries to protect and nurture their union. If the family isn't accepting of their relationship, the couple may have to love certain family members from afar until *or if* they come around.

It's important for the couple to understand that two histories are joining together. Your spouse/significant other's family and your family values may differ. Have a conversation about each of your positions within your family.

What have you participated in? Are you the driver for an elderly family member? Do you attend family dinners on a certain day of the week/month? Ask questions instead of assuming. Ask about "the elephant in the room," or what appears to be uncomfortable. Be honest and upfront about what your needs are. What can you live and not live with and why?

Consider what may and may not work in your relationship. Discuss what would be the best fit for your relationship. I also believe that the only participants in your relationship should be the couple and God (Higher power/faith/purpose). Although family, friends, and organizations mean well, their opinions, for whatever reason, may not be the best fit to enhance a healthy relationship. Seeking advice from non-biased trained professionals and those who are successful in their relationships may be helpful. At the end of the day, the final decision rests with the couple.

Your Story

Take an inventory of your current relationships. Are you the one always giving? Is it a win-win on all sides? How do you feel about the relationship(s)? (Example: Spouse, friend, partner, work, business...)

____

____

____

____

____

____

____

____

Do your relationships make you a better you? Do they make you feel responsible for their successes or failures? Do you feel that you must be their savior thereby being a crutch? (Example: Spouse, friend, partner, work, business …)

____

____

____

____

____

____

____

How can you apply what you have learned to your current experience today? (Example: I can love others from a distance if necessary…)

____

____

____

____

____

What is a note of gratitude that you can give that brought you to this point in your life? (I am thankful that I attract relationships that are for my highest good…)

Love Your Neighbor as Yourself

Mark 12:31 (The Message Bible) "And here is the second (commandment): 'Love others as well as you love yourself.' There is no other commandment that ranks with these."

I believe Mark 12:31 to be one of the necessary foundations of love. So often, I read and heard love as, loving God first and your neighbor second. However, the part that has been often overlooked is, "as you love yourself." We must love ourselves first before we can love others properly. We must have something within us before we can share it. The questions then become: What do we have in ourselves that we can share with others? Do we have the necessary ingredients? What are we giving away?

I found the following passenger emergency flight instructions helpful; "During the loss of cabin pressure, an oxygen mask will drop down from the overhead compartment. If you are traveling with young children or other people needing assistance, place your oxygen mask on first, then put the mask on the children or person needing assistance.

As humans, we seek a relationship with others. We cannot live on earth without being in relationships with people. It is a significant part of our divine design. Usually, everything humanity does involve a relationship. There are different categories of relationships, such as family, friendships, romantic, business, etc. Using research and personal experience, we will attempt to expound on love relationships. Usually, whenever we hear the word "relationship," it has become commonplace to think of romance and marriage.

Maybe it would help to shed a more light on love.

What is love?

In order to love, we must know what it is and how to apply it. Love should be a win-win event. Love has been defined in a few ways by the following sources:

According to Miriam-Webster, love is:

1) "Strong affection for another arising out of kinship or personal ties (maternal love for a child).
2) Attraction based on sexual desire: affection and tenderness felt by lovers.
3) Affection based on admiration, benevolence, or common interests (love for his old schoolmates).
   a. unselfish loyal and benevolent concern for the good of another: <u>such as</u>
      1) The fatherly concern of God for humankind
      2) brotherly concern for others
   b. A person's adoration of God.

<u>1 Corinthians 13:4-7 (NIV)</u> states; 4. Love is patient, love is kind. It does not envy, it does not boast, it is not proud. 5. It does not dishonor others, it is not self-seeking, it is not easily angered, it keeps no record of wrongs. 6. Love does not delight in evil but rejoices with the truth. 7. It always protects, always trusts, always hopes, always perseveres.

"Love does not consist of gazing at each other, but in looking outward together in the same direction." Honoré de Balzac

"What is love but acceptance of the other, whatever he is." Stendhal

"Compassion and love are not mere luxuries. As the source both of inner and external peace, they are fundamental to the continued survival of our species." Dalai Lama XIV

Hurting people hurt people. "Love your neighbor as yourself (Mark 12:31)." Before you can love others, it is imperative that you love yourself. When you do not love yourself first, others may suffer from the negativity (garbage) you dump on them. To help others, you must help yourself first. If you are hurting, get healing and strength before trying to help another hurting person. In other words, whatever areas in your life that need to be worked on, get the work done so you can be better productive to yourself and to humanity. How we feel affects our environment.

One of the most beautiful confessions I heard from a loved one was, "I'm happy that I'm in love with a man (my husband) who loves me back." I witnessed her spouse loving her through many years of illness. Love is out there, but it starts within. You must expect love and love yourself first. Too often, people try to make others responsible for making them happy. The truth is we are accountable for our happiness. If you are not happy before you get married, getting married will not make you happy.

"The husband is designed to fulfill his purpose; his purpose determines his nature, and his nature determines his needs. If you want your husband to function effectively, then discover and learn to fulfill his needs." "Don't give your spouse what you need. You both have totally opposite needs and will only frustrate each other by assuming the other should be satisfied with what satisfies you." Dr. Myles Munroe, Sr.

Loving your neighbor as yourself and doing unto others as you have them do to you, does not mean loving them the ways you want to be love. It means loving them in the way they receive the love that serves their betterment. There are five love languages, Words of affirmation, Acts of Service, Receiving Gifts, Quality Time, and Physical Touch. Although, as humans we possess them all, there are specific love languages and gifts that are more dominant in us than others. Those dominant areas applicable to each person are how they feel loved.

I believe an excellent example of loving people/organizations according to who they are in relation to their designed purpose, love language, gifting, and mission, includes but is not limited to:

If your partner enjoys vanilla ice cream and you get vanilla ice cream for them, your consideration and thoughtfulness may speak volumes. They may feel appreciated and loved, etc. On-the-other-hand, if you got him/her chocolate ice cream that you know they do not enjoy may not be received as love. Maybe it was convenient for you, and you believed that "it was the thought that counts." You possibly felt that he/she should be grateful and eat it anyway. A realistic, as opposed to an expected outcome, could result in the person getting offended, not eating the chocolate ice cream, and not feeling appreciated or heard. Your perception and actions could lead to a less than expected outcome (lack of trust, separation, resentment, fighting, etc.).

5 Secrets to a Successful Long-Term Relationship or Marriage Article by John M. Grohol, Psy.D. November 7, 2007, wrote in 5 Secrets to a Successful Long-Term Relationship or Marriage, "Compromise - Relationships are about not only taking but also giving. If you find yourself not giving very much or feeling resentful of how much you give and how little you receive back, you may be in an unequal relationship where one side takes more than they are giving. For instance, couples sometimes mistakenly believe that "love" will help them deal with any issue that comes up, and that if the other person truly loved you, they would just do as you ask. But people are independent with their own unique needs and personalities. Just because we found someone, we want to spend our lives with doesn't mean we give up our own identity in the process."

If loving someone causes you pain and illness, loving them from afar may serve you both better. That could mean social distancing yourself (separation or divorce). Remaining in a troublesome marriage for the children's sake, religious, financial reasons, and other people's opinion can hurt more than help. The potential suffering from stress, illness, multiple surgeries, thinning hair, and weight gain hurts to your detriment. You could be loving yourself to death. It is insanity. Albert Einstein says, "Insanity is doing the same thing over and over again and expecting different results."

You may have to work on your dreams before and after work. It may require you to get up extra early or go to bed late to work on yourself. A change of attitude towards the positive can change a negative situation into a positive outcome. There were a few jobs I held that I was not excited to go to each day. I did not feel specific tasks were assisting me in my purpose and fulfilling my dreams. I would complain about what was wrong with operations, leadership, etc. I realized that complaining and a negative attitude was not helping my situation. I decided to make changes within myself, thoughts, and actions.

First, I had to change my attitude. I began to say that the less exciting jobs were my "dream fund investors." I began to see my supervisors, managers, and colleagues as my support team, cheering me on. I smiled, knowing that it gets better, and I am living my dream by any means necessary. I also accepted that every event is temporary, and when complete, I would move on to the next more significant opportunity. I created my commandment that states, "I Cynthia am living a fulfilled life! Each day, I am living my dream!"

Sometimes, there is a fallacy in thinking that people can change people. Please be advised that we cannot change people. Change takes place in a person with their permission, acceptance, and willingness to comply with the change.

In my personal experience, I found it necessary at times in my life to seek assistance and get help. I spoke to clergy, life coaches, mentors, and professionals who were assigned or licensed to provide counsel. I had to find what worked for me. If I sensed or did not feel specific methods or counseling was a fit for me, I searched until I found what worked best for me. Just because a person works in a particular profession or organization does not mean their method is for you. Since we are all unique individuals, we need customized techniques to assist in our healing and betterment. Have you ever noticed that individual leaders, organizations, and schools, etc., have standardization techniques?

Those techniques used to run their organization, business, group, cookie-cutter methods, etc., are stated to be the cure-all to your problems. Some even guarantee that it will work.

However, they mostly provide a disclaimer that says something to this effect, "if it does not work, you can get your money back within/after 30 days." Every method does not work for everyone. Not all medicines work for everyone. That is why medicine is a continued practice. Certain medicines evoke sensitivities or adverse reactions. I encourage you to do what works for you. There will be naysayers, especially those you love, that may try to condemn you. People may turn away from you. The rejection may hurt and cause you to question your decision and withdraw.

Frequently it may be hard to see the positive when all you have known is negative. "You can't see the forest for the trees."

There may be times when you are in a situation that you can't make sense of and decide to accept it as the norm when deep down inside, something is telling you, "it's not right." You may be immune to a particular way of life that you considered as usual. However, once you step outside of your current questionable situation, you may be able to see clearly.

Living in DC for the first seventeen years in life made me feel that I had a handle on life. I thought the only nationalities in the world were what I saw in DC growing up, including the nationalities from the Bible. It was not until I joined the Navy and arrived at my first duty station in San Diego, CA, where I saw a rainbow of people that did not look like the few nationalities I came to know as the norm.

There was a melting pot of multiple nationalities from various parts of the world. Who knew such a rainbow of beautiful human beings existed? Leaving Washington, DC, and eventually arriving in San Diego afforded me that rich opportunity. My experience was like being in a candy shop with an assortment of multiple flavors to be explored. I got to meet and befriend many people different from me. Even more beautiful, I saw the acceptance of mixed marriages and free will of dress, etc. I saw people being themselves and loved it. In my case, marriage to my then spouse and the Navy were the vehicles that ushered me from the forest. I could see a new world to explore. I saw the trees from the forest.

It is my personal belief that there are different levels and stages of love. Sometimes, there may be a fallacy of thinking that certain people just don't measure up to our standard of love. Although that may be true, let's look at it differently. It's not that the person doesn't measure up. It may be that they are not or no longer a match to where you are going.

Maybe you have outgrown each other in various areas. You or they are where you are or can handle at that time. Misunderstandings often occur, and we may try to change the person into who we think they should be. Some examples would be: "You should be a doctor." "You should retire from a job that will give good benefits." "You should wear your hair this way." You should join our church or organization." "You should marry this person." The list goes on.

The fact of the matter is, we cannot change anyone. We can only change ourselves. Being nonjudgmental, sending love and well wishes for others in their "sinful state" so-to-speak is one of the best examples that demonstrate love. This approach may speak volumes to the not so lovable and encourage them to look at themselves.

Have you ever felt ugly or inferior? I heard a comedian say that **"ugly"** stands for y**o**u **g**ot to love **y**ourself! What matters is what you think and choose to believe about yourself. Programs, programs, programs are all around, waiting to infiltrate our minds and very well-being. It's our choice what we allow into our minds and hearts. We have been conditioned to first look for the so-called wrong or flaw in a thing or person before seeing their true beauty. Commercials and propaganda have told society how to think and look. Societal body dictates "the perfect" unrealistic physique not attainable by all. Beauty has been classified as the perfect hour-glass shape for women and the muscular inverted triangle for men. We have gone on diets and exercise programs to meet the status-quo. Some have even died for it. Some of those who have attained the alleged perfect bodies have reverted to their previous situations with greater disappointments or revolving emptiness. I'm not saying that being in the best physical shape for physical longevity to live your purpose is wrong. There are many body types, designs, and capabilities. One size does not fit all. Psalms 139:14 says that we are fearfully and wonderfully made. We are created with a certain uniqueness.

We are equally created human beings as originals with designated gifts and purposes. We all have certain avenues we must travel to complete our purpose and goals. Since God (Source) who created us says we are perfect, who are we to say otherwise? I enjoy reading Louise Hay, "You Can Heal Your Life." I also like reciting the positive affirmations she wrote "I approve of myself. I am worth loving. I now begin accepting myself as I am…" She also has a mirror exercise where you look at yourself in the mirror and practice saying good things about yourself. We must first love and accept our beauty and uniqueness with confidence.

1. In 1970, despite having to and enduring racial discrimination, prejudices, unfair practices, and segregation, Carl Brashear was the first African-American to become a U.S. Navy Master Diver (Master Chief Petty Officer/E9). He would later win his case to remain in Naval service with an amputated leg.

2. Regardless of not having an organization mentor and or the highest evaluation marks, in 2003, I Cynthia (Farmer) Prospers became the first Administration department woman of color to advance to the rank of United States Navy Chief Petty Officer in the history of Electronic Attack Squadron 209 (VAQ-209).

3. Kyle Maynard is a speaker, author, and ESPY award-winning mixed martial arts athlete known for becoming the first quadruple amputee to ascend Mount Kilimanjaro without the aid of prosthetics.

4. Helen Keller, became deaf, dumb, and blind shortly after birth. Despite her greatest misfortune, she has written her name indelibly in the pages of the history of the great. Her entire life has served as evidence that no one ever is defeated until defeat had been accepted as a reality (Napoleon Hill)."

It has been my experience that some of my elevations and successes came in the final hours or moments before what appeared to be the making or breaking points.

<u>Enlightenment:</u>

"Everyday, think as you wake up, today I am fortunate to be alive, I have a precious human life, I am not going to waste it. I am going to use all my energies to develop myself, to expand my heart out to others, to achieve enlightenment for the benefit of all beings. I am going to have kind thoughts towards others. I am not going to get angry or think badly about others. I am going to benefit others as much as I can." Dalai Lama XIV

By this time, you may have recognized that most of the change is in dealing with yourself and less in trying to change others. Working on you and your rescue is very important. Love your neighbor as you love yourself. Take care of yourself, be you, and love you. Begin to receive love by loving yourself first. "Love your neighbor as you love yourself."

Love yourself enough to live your purpose. Do not allow anyone, be it family, church, etc. stop you from living your purpose. We are responsible for getting our earthly assignment done. While you are serving others, be mindful of serving yourself too. I have seen people put their dreams, goals, and purpose on hold to assist others with their vision. Many have died with unfulfilled dreams, goals, purpose, etc.

"The greatest tragedy in life is not death, but a life without a purpose." Myles Munroe, Sr.

Using what does not work for you can hurt you. It is essential to find what is useful for you. If a person, organization, or group is hurting you (threats, demeaning, physical, mental, spiritual harm) and you dread participating with them, I recommend social distancing yourself from them and seek help that heals and builds you up. Total healing may not happen overnight. It may take some time for you to be free.

Exercise:

The following techniques are credited to and inspired by Louise Hay.

1. Look in the mirror and say to yourself, "I love you (say your name)."

If you cannot or feel uncomfortable saying, "I love you" to yourself, ask yourself why. It is important not to get angry with yourself. You may think of a time or event that made you feel negative about yourself. It could have been something that someone influential in your life said to or about you. It could be from an event that caused you pain. Assistance is available. I encourage you to seek out experienced professionals such as counselor's, psychologists, abuse hotlines, and local community resources and services, self-help books and support groups, etc.

2. Forgive those who have offended or hurt you. Stand in front of a mirror and pretend that person is in front of you. Forgive them for hurting you and not being what you expected them to be.

3. Forgive yourself for getting offended and seeing yourself as inferior.

4. Say out loud to yourself in front of the mirror, "I approve of myself, and I am enough."

5. Compliment your body from head-to-toe.

6. Think of something beautiful to say about all the people you encounter.

7. Say something nice about people who were not kind or loving to you.

What are some ways that you can love yourself (Example: I looked in the mirror and complimented myself, I exercised today…)?

____

____

____

____

____

____

____

____

In what way did you love your neighbor as yourself? (Example: Compliment friend, partner…)

____

____

____

____

____

____

How can you apply what you have learned to your current experience today?

____

____

____

____

____

____

What is a note of gratitude that you can give that brought you to this point in your life? (I am thankful that I attract relationships that are for my highest good…)

____

____

____

____

____

____

____

Dating and Going Beyond the Walls

Sometimes we set boundaries and will not travel outside of a certain area for convenience. Maybe you desire a relationship and wish to be married, and the best person for you may live more than a couple of hours outside your local area. You may have already placed your order. "I'll have a man who is 6 ft. 5 in, tall, dark, handsome, rich, etc." "I want a woman who is beautiful, curvy, plump, spiritual, intelligent, etc." "Oh yeah, they must live in my area within 25 miles.

These orders may be due to limiting beliefs that have held us back. The right person for you may differ from the order you placed. That person may be the very person we need to add to our purpose and happiness. "Doing the same thing over and over and expecting different results" is referred to as insanity. Sometimes you must go beyond the limits to get the very person who will propel you and that person into accomplishing a greater purpose.

Now that we know what we know or are old enough to find out the excuse, "This isn't how I was raised…," is obsolete. More than likely, it is some of our "upbringing" that could have sabotaged our relationships. After all, our parents didn't know what they didn't know.

So, what now? Again, I hear the promises of this and that, and it seemed like expectations amounted to nothing. What do you do when you think you have made it, only to be presented yet again with another challenge? "What do you do," is a good question to ask. Do I try and do it on my own, or do I trust in God (Source)? Where is the light at the end of the tunnel? Where is the pot of gold at the end of the rainbow? When do you know that you have made it? Is it just one challenge after another?

We have to first be the change we want to see. We have to be the characteristics and the character that we want in our mate. We have to be that first. It's important to work on ourselves until he or she arrives. It may appear, that person may not have everything that you think he or she should have.

It's possible that those few things are being cultivated. You may see the majority of what you desire or need in a suitable mate. However, if we say they are a little too round, they are too short, he/she is the wrong complexion, or they can't balance a checkbook… Could it be that those little things can be caught? Can it be that the little things will come during the uniting of the two? Every part of the body is important. When the body is fitly joined together, there is agreement. "From him, the whole body, joined and held together by every supporting ligament, grows and builds itself up in love, as each part does its work (Eph 4:16 NIV)."

In other words, when the right one for you appears, height, weight, complexion, the school they attended should not be a factor from which you make your decision. Here are some factors to consider, love, spirituality, respect, agreement, support, security, positive self-esteem, compassion, availability, ability, cultivation, and remaining a lifetime learner in continued development (spiritual, mental, physical, and emotional). This does not include abuse of any kind (spiritual, physical, verbal, mental, and emotional) or anything that can harm you or the other person.

I believe the answer to the above questions are for us to just live our purpose and continue on our designated path. Sometimes there are detours. I believe that with every detour or pause, there is a lesson to be learned as well. There are times when people have been scolded for being on the wrong path or missing the mark (sin) according to their interpretation. Have we really missed the mark? That is the mystery question. Maybe or maybe not.

However, we are all born with a purpose, and how we get there may not be the prescribed plan of the status quo. The status quo gives us a particular box to reside in. One example would be the so-called "American Dream" to go to college, get a good job, get married, buy a three-bedroom house with a white picket fence and have two or three children… Listen, it doesn't always happen that way.

People sometimes have to take detours. Some people live in project housing, commonly known as "the ghetto." Some people are homeless… Everyone was not born with a silver spoon in their mouth. Where or who you were born to doesn't determine your greatness. What you do with what you have determines your greatness. Our story and victory come out of the journey.

Her Story

Concerning "dating and going beyond the walls," I was all for it. I did not want to date or marry anyone from my hometown. I believed that I heard all the tired pick-up lines. I was avoiding "*Charlie men* (see the "Three Types of Men" page 93) or spoiled boys" who wanted "mommas" to take care of them financially while ruling as a so-called king.

After working on myself and being the change, I wanted to see, I met and married my late husband Donald Brooks, who was living in my hometown. Wow, God has a sense of humor. My first meeting with him was interesting and disturbing. I thought he was a loudmouth, arrogant man *like the rest of the men in my town.* In taking offense to some things he said, I had to ask myself why I took offense.

I asked myself what in me resembled what he said. After finding what those things were, I was able to listen to him from a place of non-judgment and heard his heart. I found that he was a caring humanitarian with a sense of humor, etc. He was the right man for me during his remaining time on earth. It seemed like everything we touched together turned to gold and happened at exponential speed. I learned to be non-judgmental and check within myself first. I was reminded to remain open to the great possibilities.

His Story

Sometimes people unwillingly build walls concerning their goals, aspirations, and wants. In a way, it limits their reach to achieve those necessary things. Sometimes you have to expand your reach and your ability to go beyond the walls of your limitations. Certain goals are achieved in life by unwillingly going past your expectations and perceived paths and roads that you have set for yourself.

I know that some of the goals I have achieved were not planned. They were by accident or came from my passion for different things. My love of people, and life, brought an individual in my life that normally I would not have purposely looked for. They had to also go past the walls of limitation that they had set for themselves concerning what or who they wanted.

Sometimes our greatest gift of growth comes from stumbling, stumbling in the sense of tripping over ourselves or the goals and limitations we placed on ourselves. Sometimes growth is just like the discovery of penicillin. It came from the growth on molded bread. It was an unconscious effort. It was by mistake and became one of the greatest discoveries to cure diseases, make vaccines, and so many other curable items. It wasn't a planned thing. Sometimes we can plan so much that we miss out on life's real purposes.

Enlightenment:

There are people looking up to and depending on you. They are expecting you to make it and there are some hoping that you fail. Let that tenacious drive within you push you to keep going towards your vision, dreams, and goals. Sometimes it may appear that you come up empty or have wasted time. "I could have been somewhere else." Rather than think of what could or should have been, choose to be in the "now."

I believe that every person and thing serve a season in our purpose. I have no regrets. I just keep moving forward. When I finish one assignment, another one is presented. More often than not, the next assignment is presented before the completion of the current one.

The secret is to remain teachable/coachable. Change must first begin within. We produce what we are. It is our inherent nature to follow leaders who have what we want. Therefore, we surround ourselves with and study people who inspire us. Learning life lessons provide us with a foundation to enrich the world. I believe lessons make the world better and give others hope to let them know that they can make it and that there is purpose and that there is joy in living your purpose.

What qualities do you need in a mate? (Example: I need a mate who is caring, tenacious, etc.)

____

____

____

____

____

____

____

____

What same qualities you possess that you desire in a mate? (Ex: I am nurturing and caring…)

____

____

____

____

____

____

____

____

____

What are some adjustments do you need to make within yourself? (What I'm doing over and over again which is not working…, I need to listen actively.)

____

____

____

____

____

____

____

____

In what ways have you gone beyond your limiting beliefs? (Instead of asking for muscular/curvy mate, I can ask for a loving mate that is the best mate for me …)

____

____

Shelf-Life

"There is a time for everything, and a season for every activity under the heavens:" Ecclesiastes 3:1(NIV)

I believe all creation has a shelf-life in one form or another. Imagine food items. Fresh food has to be eaten within a prescribed time in order to receive the full benefits of its provision. Lettuce is better eaten fresh and crispy. Waiting too long will cause the lettuce to be wilted and dull.

It appears that the tongue longs for the crispy, crunchy texture and refreshing hydration lettuce give. It compliments sandwiches and salads… Canned food items are packaged and designed to be consumed in a certain amount of time. If those items aren't consumed within the prescribed recommended time, they lose flavor, nutrients, etc.

We were born with gifts and talents that are meant to be used here on earth. Gifts and talents are not for the sweet by and by. They are for the here and now. They must be cultivated and used to help add increase to other people's lives. There is a saying, "you lose what you don't use." If you were born to sing, then sing. If you were born to teach, then teach, etc. Our talents, abilities and gifts need to be exercised to translate appropriately.

Every person was already born with their purpose inside of them. Everything we need is already inside of us. Look in and accept with thanksgiving our designed future as now. We were born rich with the prescribed outcome. Imagine an apple that is cut in half. What do you see?

You should see the seeds in the middle of the apple. The seeds have been program by its creator. The seeds say that the apple is an apple orchard (a piece of land planted with apple trees). Its legacy is to be a producer of many apple orchards/groves. Its legacy is to provide continuous life-giving fruit to forthcoming generations. Its future is already inside of it.

His Story

Sometimes we don't recognize the expiration period. Staying in an unhealthy marriage too long will begin to mentally and physically eat away at you. That's because you stayed past the shelf life of that marriage. We may stay past the shelf life of our jobs or such. We make these decisions based on *fear*, financial needs… It can have a negative effect on different areas of our life.

Enlightenment:

Our future is already inside of us. We must look within. Get going and act. Money isn't needed to get started. Get started, and the money will come.

What is/are your gift(s)/talent(s)?

How does your gift(s)/talent(s) serve your purpose?

How do I feel about other people's opinions?

____

____

____

____

____

____

____

How are the opinions of those serving you?

____

____

____

____

____

____

____

Respect Your Elders

Respecting our elders is more than just speaking kindly to them or giving head of the line privilege, visiting the elderly in retirement homes, and listening to their stories. Elders are designed by God to pour wisdom into the next generation that will benefit many generations to come. They must transfer the legacy that will help empower the generations that will come after them.

Thank you elders, (parents)Ernest, Mattie and Brenda, (grandparents) Earnest, Mattie, George and May, (aunts/uncles) Inez, Lula Mae, Bill, Charlene, John, Mable, Marie... for preparing me for my life's purpose.

Blessing from a Matriarch

It was in the east where I was ordained and received speaking invitations and coaching service requests. I was able to minister to and bond with distant family members I had not seen or visited since I was a young girl. I had numerous opportunities to visit with the most senior member of my family, Aunt Winnie. She was 107 years young in 2019 to include being witty, loveable, very alert, and not mincing her words. Aunt Winnie never failed to tell me her story and family history.

She was truly a joy to listen to. I made it a priority to touch base with her to glean from her wisdom and hear her pray audibly as she blessed our family and others and imparted our legacy. She was a true trailblazer who has paved the way for our family. Through her, I met other family members I would have never met if it wasn't for her historic 100th birthday celebration. She was the vehicle. Aunt Winnie is well known throughout our entire family and made the time to visit our family throughout the United States. Here is a prayer Aunt Winnie prayed after I asked her to pray for our family and me. Me: "Can you pray for me as you sometimes do?" Aunt Winnie: "Oh, okay, a short prayer?" Me: "Yes, Ma'am." Aunt Winnie: "Ok." She prays, "Father, I come before you this morning. Thank you, Lord, we were having fellowship with my lovely niece, and Lord it has been a blessing, and now is the time she asked me to pray for her, and I don't know the situation; but Lord, whatever her needs are, you know her needs and I pray for her, and I pray for her husband and for the children and for the whole family. Father bless my niece. Whatever her need is, your will-will be done in her heart, in her life.

Thank you for her. Bless her. Now, I submit her unto you. I pray for her whole family that she will have a good year from now until Christmas. Not only that, just take care of her and her family. Thank you in Jesus precious name, Amen."

When I departed from the west coast, the provision/brook was drying up so to speak. Therefore, it was necessary for me to pack and return to the east coast. Opportunity came knocking, and I had to answer the *door* and follow the voice of my spirit (intuition). There are times when we must move to higher ground to sustain our purpose. Fluidity and flexibility are essential on our journey to refreshment and success. I know I am a winner. I don't know the "how". On-the-other- hand, the "how" is not my business. Wherever I go is where I am needed at that time. I am enjoying being fluid. I'm enjoying life, living my purpose, as well as helping others identify and take steps towards living theirs. I am thankful for the surplus to live an abundant life. I can't take anything with me. I came into this world naked without physical belongings, and that's the way I'll leave this earth. We don't own anything here on this earth. We are stewards over them. We are borrowing them. They can only be used in this earthly realm. "The earth is the Lords and the fullness thereof, the world and those who dwell therein (Psalm 24:1)."

We can't take our luxury cars, houses, designer clothes, etc. On this note, I remember sorting through my mother's things when she transitioned. She had some things hidden that she didn't want anyone to find. I found them. As long as she was here in her physical body, she could manage them. However, once she passed away, they were no longer her concern. They remained here and were given to and shared among other people. Some of her things/treasures were old, rusted, moth-eaten, stolen, and she couldn't do anything about it. Her departure took her to a new location with its applicable provisions.

We must be aware that not all vehicles are the physical motorized modus-operandi. Some of the vehicles I had to use may not have been the ones I would have chosen. Some of them included temporarily living with other people and their rules, residing in opulent or less desirable places, being bi-vocational, etc. These vehicles were essential in reaching my goals. I've learned that there is a set time to be in each location of life. Some of the times can range from short to long-term, depending upon my intended purpose and accomplishments.

Ma's Legacy

I always heard my mother give gratitude to God. She also encouraged us (her children) to pray to God for what we need. She would say, "Pray about it." Mother dubbed this phrase from her mother. I guess when you hear something said long enough, you'll begin to say it too. She always had a "things to do list," goals list, and before her passing, a book of possibilities. Ma received some of the things that were on her lists that I could physically see.

Her latest desires besides oxygen were yet to be received. In fact, she received about half of her desires from her possibilities book. I must say that her lack of receipt unsettled me to the point of ensuring that I reach my goals and desires. These findings were a catalyst in my focusing on the end results.

I was led to look at the house where my mother lived as a little girl with her siblings, parents, and Aunt Shug. I thought to myself how great it would be if I could get the opportunity to go inside the house. As I arrived, I saw the house had a for rent sign in the yard. I was excited and took a flyer of the house that included pictures. I also called the realtor and made an appointment to go inside. Taking it a step further, I contacted family members to give them the opportunity to see where a part of our beginnings was. I was interested in getting some of my mother's remaining siblings in there, who would tell the stories and the significance of each room.

I successfully got my aunt, the youngest of my grandmother's children, along with my eldest brother, to accompany me. We listened to our aunt as she began the storytelling. As we entered the yard, she told stories about being in the yard. Next, she told a story about the steps and the front doors.

She had a story for each room of the house and the many family members who lived there. Auntie told the stories from her perspective with such passion that made us feel like we were there. There wasn't any door, room, closet, or corner that was left out. Auntie brought the house to life. My brother and I laughed at the stories, which included the antics of our mother.

There were two of a few stories that had us laughing hysterically. One of the stories was of my mother being late to school every morning although she lived next door to the school, and the other was of Blackie, the family dog who ate her food that she had left on the table. Her plan to return to eat her food was an epic failure as Blackie licked the plate clean as she entered the room. This three-level brownstone housed many of our family and extended family members.

Another story included stolen banana pudding and desserts my cousin would leave on the window seal to cool. Not only did we hear the funny stories, were also heard the stories of loss and rebuilding. Throughout all the storytelling, I could hear the sound of hope, faith, and belief that they would overcome and win. I could hear my family's work ethic and togetherness. This house on 5th Street became the refuge and transition house for some of our family member that relocated to Washington, DC. from South Carolina and other locations.

Being a caretaker for my mom as I watched her health fail rapidly was painful. I saw the throws of death surround her, waiting to usher her to the next life. I was not ready for that dreaded call stating that Ma had passed away just after the midnight hour. My heart felt like it dropped out of my body onto the floor. I felt like I had just delivered a baby.

Soon afterward, I heard the horrible sound of an out of tune bassoon. It was the sound of groanings that could not be uttered. I quickly realized it was me. My younger children were startled and awakened by my groanings as my body went limp.

The month prior to my mom's passing, I was angry because I could not write a $32,000 check to a natural holistic health hospital that specialized in treating my mother's terminal condition with successful results. I was experiencing mixed feelings that she could still be here and then realizing that she is no longer suffering. I was angry because her doctor assured me that the clinic would be getting a certain cyberknife machine by a certain date that he could have tried on her.

I decided to do some research for treatment centers that may be able to treat her and found that the hospital already had the machine in their cancer treatment center. They had the machine close to her date of medical diagnosis and possibly could have used it then. However, it was not used.

Understanding that medicine is a practice, why was it not used? Could it be her type of insurance? Could it be that she was in a certain test pool? After meeting with her doctor, who then sent her home to be comfortable and die, I informed him of my research and findings. He had a surprised look on his face. My interpretation was that he probably didn't think I would do research and just take his word for it.

I also learned that for whatever reason, she didn't tell her immediate family that the illness had reappeared. By the time we found out, it was a race against the clock. She reached out to me for help, and there was nothing I could do. During and after Ma's rapid illness, I had gotten frustrated with a few of my siblings and seriously considered writing them off. I didn't feel they were doing enough concerning our mother's care.

My thought was to distance myself from them due to a difference of opinions that we had shared. If I distanced myself from them, I would not have to be bothered with them until the next life event, whatever that may be. After settling my mother's estate, my siblings came to me and thanked me for taking the lead in my mother's care and estate. They expressed that they didn't have the strength to assist in certain areas as they were used to seeing our mother as strong and independent.

Her Story

One night, I dreamed that my mother had a baby girl and gave her to us (her five children) before she transitioned (died). The characters in my dream were my siblings and myself; my cousin's fiancée; a couple of male family members who felt they had a sense of entitlement; an Orange Anaconda snake with dark orange or red patterns; a young man from a previous childhood church I attended…

There was an orange anaconda snake with dark orange or red pattern that seemed to be familiar with my sister and me as if we had carried it before.

We obviously courted this snake and realized we could no longer carry it and allow it to hinder us. We carried it in a shopping cart and allowed it to sit in the front seat of our vehicle. It was watching for us and made a squealing sound and was sitting coiled. I noticed the snake before it saw me, and I went to another part of the parking lot undetected by the snake to get into another vehicle. Someone assisted me in my getaway.

I then walked into this building with automatic doors. My sister was holding the baby and trying to get me to hold her. However, I told her that I was busy and had work to do and said that I would hold her when I can. She placed the baby on her back on the bed lengthwise as she sat at the end of the bed watching television with my older brother. My older brother was sitting in a chair to the left of her.

My youngest brother was there briefly as he was in the military. As I was walking past the bed with the baby on it, I decided to pick her up. I was horrified to find that she was stiff and had stopped breathing. I began to cry, "the baby's not moving." "She's not breathing." I began to speak to the baby, "I love you; I want you; you are wanted."

My eldest brother said to me, "let me see her." As I was beginning to hand her over to him, she began to breathe again and became limber. I kept holding her in my arms and began caressing her and patting her back as I held her close to my heart. After she was loved, I placed her in a baby carrier and placed her on a higher platform.

I had left her for a brief moment and was keeping an eye on her. She began to cry. I looked over at her as I was walking towards her and saw her looking over the right side of the carrier and was beginning to fall. I ran towards her and caught her before she could fall from the carrier. I told her, "don't cry, I love you." I then began singing this song I never heard before:

"I love Jesus yes, I do. I love Jesus because the Bible tells me to. I love Jesus; yes, I do. I love Jesus, and I love you."

My younger brother had walked into the space complaining about the unfairness he was receiving at his construction job. I began encouraging him to be thankful for his job and to see it in another light. He was wearing a burlap waist apron with a gold satin slip hanging from it. I told him that his slip was showing. I thought he would be discreet and pull it out of sight, and I began laughing. He then transformed into this awesome young man I attended church with which was around his age. The young man is a very spiritual successful entrepreneur.

My cousin's fiancée said she was going to the store to get some things when some family members arrived, and I addressed them as "kinfolk." They were from "around the way" and rang the doorbell. I answered the door. It was a male with three other males. I said, "Yes, can I help you?" The lead male pushed the door open and said, "just let me in." They were talking about getting profits from a project or something. Afterward, I was at the store with a family member who asked me to purchase something, and I asked why. She said that it was because she had already purchased a lot of stuff with her money. She expected me to pitch-in and not the other people who were partaking in the festivity. I was a bit taken aback and felt ambushed. After all, I was working within a budget also, and the dream ended.

You're trying to let the legacy live. A snake will try to choke out and kill the legacy. Family tries to do it through words and actions.

<u>Enlightenment:</u>

The baby was our mother's legacy, which she left us her children to carry on. If we fail to carry her legacy, it will die. Although there may be distractions (snake, family and situations) trying to prevent us, we must do our part and carry it out. The Lord has strategically placed people and various forms of help (get-away car) to assist us and Ma's life-giving legacy. The song was gratitude to the Great I AM in saying I Love Jesus and then to our mother's Legacy saying I Love the Legacy (You). The Legacy is passed down from my grandmother to my mother; "Just pray about it," and "Seek the Kingdom of God First and his righteousness and All these things shall be added to you (Matt 6:33)." I caught the legacy before it could fall to the ground. Joel, my younger brother, and I saw it. He saw it from within and called for a meeting. I saw it from without.

4 "There are different kinds of spiritual gifts, but they are all from the same Spirit. 5 There are different ways to serve, but we serve the same Lord. 6 And there are different ways that God works in people, but it is the same God who works in all of us to do everything.

7 Something from the Spirit can be seen in each person. The Spirit gives this to each one to help others. 8 The Spirit gives one person the ability to speak with wisdom. And the same Spirit gives another person the ability to speak

with knowledge. 9 The same Spirit gives faith to one person, and to another, he gives gifts of healing. 10 The Spirit gives to one person the power to do miracles, to another the ability to prophesy, and to another the ability to judge what is from the Spirit and what is not. The Spirit gives one person the ability to speak in different kinds of languages, and to another the ability to interpret those languages. 11 One Spirit, the same Spirit, does all these things. The Spirit decides what to give each one. 1 Corinthians 12:4-11 (ERV).”

Although there may be many siblings in the same family who received the same training, each sibling may receive the information differently. Each child has different giftings and tolerances. Each sibling has different strengths and skills. One sibling may walk or potty train quicker than another sibling. Someone may be stronger in math, and another person may excel in English. Therefore, the person who is stronger in a particular area can complete a task faster and more efficiently. The other person that does not have the same gifting may take longer to do the same task. After receiving this revelation, I realized that my siblings were not stronger in executing the necessary steps during certain times of our mother’s illness and passing. What I received from my mom as harsh treatment and excessive responsibilities prepared me for the day of her passing and final services. “This is the day that Lord has made let us rejoice and be glad in it (Psalm 118:24).” I was prepared for that day.

Whenever you are in an uncomfortable situation, you can do a mental forward projection of the good you desire. Let's consider being separated from your family for an extended period of time. See yourself embracing your loved ones and at your welcome home reception. See yourself doing fun and bonding activities with your family. Afterward, take an inventory of the emotions you would experience and feel them now. Keep the vision in front of you. Without a vision, the people perish *or lose hope...* (Proverbs 29:18).

Think of an event in your life where you may have wanted to quit. What was it? (Example: I could barely have fun because I was always taking care of my younger brother.)

____

____

____

____

____

____

____

____

How has it helped you today? (Ex: I am nurturing and caring…)

____

____

____

____

____

____

____

____

What was your enlightening moment? (I had to be my mother's caregiver as she was dying.)

____

____

____

____

____

____

____

What is a note of gratitude that you can give that brought you to this point in your life? (I am thankful that I was fully available to take care of my mother in her final moments…)

____

Being the Sermon

"If your religion causes you not to love others, you need to get a new religion."
Donald Brooks

One of the greatest moments in my life was being ordained and the events that would follow.

Pentecost Sunday, May 24, 2015, at Truth and Life Christian Church under the leadership of Senior Pastor, Rev. Dr. Ella Thompson, was the point of origin for my licensed ordination into ministry.

I thanked and greeted my family and friends for being present to celebrate a new chapter in my life. I was surprised that my father, a Primitive Baptist Moderator (Bishop), would forego his own church service in North Carolina and travel to Virginia to be a part of my special day.

As I was sitting in the pew waiting for my ordination, my senior pastor informed me that my dad agreed to help with my ordination. Apparently, she asked for his assistance as I was in the dressing room putting on the purple satin robe with black and gold trim, she gave me to wear for my ordination. I never told my senior pastor that my father's denomination didn't allow women preachers. On the other hand, I'm sure daddy wasn't expecting that he would be asked to be a participant in my ordination. I only gave her his title of Elder. I'm glad for my sake, I did not share that information. That event was memorable and historical. I believe that he was in accordance with the biblical text, Galatians 3:28, "There is neither Jew nor Gentile, neither slave nor free, nor is there male and female, for you are all one in Christ Jesus."

I stood in front of my Pastor and Father. My eyes were glued on my dad as he stood in front of me and spoke blessings over me and passed me a ministry baton. I trembled as the tears flowed from my eyes. Is this Daddy speaking and imparting the blessing over me?

Daddy's presence reminded me of his coming to stay the night with me at the hospital. No one told me that the doctors said that I was going to die and wasn't expected to live through the night. I was fifteen. We had a father-daughter talk, which ended in forgiveness, love, and new beginnings. I can only imagine that daddy must have stayed up all night praying for me and pleading to God to let his baby girl live. King Daddy stood in the gap and had a talk with the Most-High King on behalf of his princess. The next morning, I woke up. Good morning Daddy! Daddy seemed to be happy. He can tell the story much better than I can. If you ever get the opportunity to hear my father speak, you'll know what I mean.

It was time for me to give my initial sermon. As I looked out into the audience, I didn't see my mother. I began to cry uncontrollably because I had then realized that this event was the first time that my mother was not physically present. She looked forward to me being ordained one day, and now she wasn't here to share it with me. I was able to compose myself and deliver my sermon. I believe Ma was with me in spirit.

I was given several opportunities to share a platform to teach a Life Class with my father. It was wonderful teaching alongside my dad, minister-to-minister, and delivering life-changing words. He delivered biblically, and I interpreted it into everyday life application through transformation coaching.

One day, I began thumbing through my book of recorded dreams. I recorded a dream dated August 16, 2010. I dreamed of my mother preaching from a short pulpit platform. She was wearing a purple satin robe with golden trim. She was preaching very well! She began making proclamations and praying for people. As I was turning to get a view of my mother in action, she placed her hand on my forehead and began to pray and proclaim blessings over me.

I was determined that I would not fall onto the ground under the anointing of the Holy Spirit. I decided to be polite and allow her to pray for me. Before I knew it, I felt the power of God (a warm, comforting and, supportive feeling of a mother) flowed from the top of my head to the soles of my feet. It was so powerful; I could no longer stand.

My spirit leaped upward from my body, and I fell backward onto the lawn.
My spirit and body lay resting in unison under the power of the Holy Spirit.
This event took place in a small fenced in backyard. It wasn't in a spectacular
setting. However, the spectacular happened. I never saw my mother wearing
this robe during her life. It dawned on me that I was wearing a similar purple
satin robe as she wore in my dream. The robe belonged to my senior pastor,
who allowed me to wear it for my ceremony. The platform height and
building size, and surroundings were like my dream. Could it be that my
mother was with me? I believe she was with me and saw my day before I did.
She passed the baton to me. In hindsight, I was my mother, and my mother
was I.

Departures and Arrivals

Moses led the Israelites out of Egypt. However, he did not lead them into the Promised Land. In fact, Joshua led them into the land of promise. There are certain people designated to get us from one place to another. Not everyone will be with us through our entire journey.

We should understand that all things are temporal and subject to change. It was intended that all the Israelites would enter the Promised Land at a particular time. However, due to the unbelief and complaining of the elders, they could not enter in. The only Israelites allowed to enter were under the age of twenty. That tells me, who I associate with long enough, I become. I become the blessing or the downfall. Note to self: "Re-evaluate my associates."

In order to go in, we have to come out from somewhere. Therefore, if we are in, we have to come out to go in. I had a certain destination to reach, which required me to first leave my home. I had to go outside of my home, get into my vehicle, and head to the destination. When I arrived at my destination, I had to get out of my car and walk towards the place where I was going. Once I arrived, I had to go in from the outside. While inside, I had to complete my purpose for being there. After my call to action and response was complete, I left to go to another destination. Sometimes we will encounter sweet, bitter, or bitter-sweet experiences. The question then becomes; "How can I learn from this or what is the take-away I am supposed to receive for the betterment of myself and others?"

We as people are meant to transition into new growth. On our journey towards our goals, visions/dreams, purpose, and destiny, there will be various types of qualifying people to help us get to where we are going. A necessary concern is the people we choose to follow. Our choices will dictate the outcome. Have you ever noticed, after arriving at your destination, the host/person may ask, "How was your trip, or did you find the address okay?" They are asking about your journey. They want to hear your triumphs that led you to the victory of your arrival. Your arrival is all about the story. What type of traffic did you encounter? Were there any incidents? Was traffic smooth and flowing? Who did you meet along the way? Did they help or hinder your process? Did you have to seek out the help of subject matter experts? Did you have to take a detour? We remember our journey for the most part. We find ourselves talking about what happened before our *successful* arrival. Some of the stories are good, and others are apparently bad.

Let us be reminded that there a certain planning and preparations that are necessary in getting us to the next location. Although some of our plans may not pan out as expected, it's better to have a plan than not to have one. The plan is a point of reference, even in the detour. Habakkuk 2:2-3 (ERV) says The Lord answered me, "Write down (the vision) what I show you. Write it clearly on a sign so that the message will be easy to read. This message is about a special time in the future. This message is about the end, and it will come true. Just be patient and wait for it. That time will come; it will not be late.

I would also encourage us to reread our vision and goals daily with the acceptance that it has already happened for us. It will manifest when we are ready for it. For example, if we want to save money, we need to get a savings account. While we are waiting for the manifestation of them, it is important that we remain active, working on ourselves to receive the promise. "Faith without works is dead (James 2:17)." "To know and not do, is to not yet know" (Confucius).

Should we forget the transportation needed to get to our destination? We always need a vehicle to take us there. This is a reminder to me. After having to relocate to several states within the U.S. I moved via bus, airplane, truck, and cars. Between 2012 to 2016, it is very interesting that I have relocated coast-to-coast more times post-military than during my military service. I moved to one location, assuming that I would be there for at least a year. Within ten months of living in that location, I was beckoned to return to reside on the east coast. I had just recently returned from the east. The trip was supposed to be four days and ended up being three and a half weeks. I must say that I thoroughly enjoyed myself. In times past, I would be ready to leave after four days to return to my home and unwind. However, this time, I desired to stay longer in my home of record, where I vowed that I would only visit. After returning to my home in the west, I received a confirmation that it was time for me to move back home. I had to finalize my affairs and "get to stepping" towards home.

It depends on when people come into your life. You have to make sure it's the right time for them to depart. You can't delay their departure, or you'll miss out on another arrival that's important for you. I almost delayed my departure a little too late, where I almost lost you (Cynthia). It was long enough so that you could come into my life so I could check to see whether you were supposed to arrive in my life. It's very important to know when to say when or when it's time to go. When you stop feeling less than or not as good as you felt before you met that person, then it's time for you to leave. Sometimes we stay because of financial, sexual, and connection reasons, etc. Once you get past those premises, it's time for them to go. That's when you find out how much strength you really have. I wanted to make sure I departed on good ground so there wouldn't be any obstructions to block my new arrival *Cynthia*. My job was to ensure that any coming obstruction was eliminated to enable a new plane to land on my runway (in my life). The departure was at the right time to allow for your arrival.

"You only do more when you get more." "You only do more when you get more." "You only do more when you get more." As you began to do more for me, you got more of my attention. Therefore, it assisted me with my departure. It's not a matter of "if," but "when."

"I was hoping that you *Cynthia* were lady-like outside of the romantic type and romantically devilish." I know we have to have certain needs met. We look for a hundred percent that really isn't a hundred percent. It may only be fifty percent that feels like 100%. Therefore, I tend to set the bar in friendship high so if there is a departure, there isn't any animosity.

Enlightenment:

In life, we will always be arriving somewhere. We will always be departing from somewhere to arrive somewhere. Do we ever arrive? I believe that we arrive in different aspects of our calling. When we arrive, we are then at the place we were supposed to get to at that time. Afterward, we depart that place to arrive in another place to complete another assignment, possibly different than the previous one.

Your Story

Do you know where you are going to? Write the vision.

Where do you want to or are led to go next? (Example: I want to go back to school… I want to move to… I'm feeling led to…)

____

____

____

____

____

____

____

____

Write it, describe it and say it out loud as if you are there now. (Ex: I am sitting in my first class and excited that I actually did this…)

____

____

____

____

____

____

____

Project yourself forward to your desired outcome. (Wow, this experience turned out better than I could have ever imagined...)

____

____

____

____

____

____

____

What is a note of gratitude that you can give that brought you to this point in your life? (I am thankful that the God/Universe opportunities and people were there to get me to this point. The "how," was taken care of.)

____

____

____

____

____

____

____

____

Redeeming the Time

My previous station in life and a divorce would take me to different places throughout the United States to assist others, work a job and reestablish myself. It seemed that no matter where I went, I felt a sense of homelessness. Although I had been married and in certain company, I felt a void. Living in other people's homes by their rules and forfeiting things I would normally do in my own space or acquiescing to other people's rules or move were the only solutions.

A respectful reaction would be to stay out of sight. When I was fortunate to get my own room, I would stay in there. However, the host/hostess knew I was still there. For the most part, I had to be on my best behavior. I began to ask myself, "What and where is home?" As my job at that time was ending, I relocated to the east coast to live with and assist my father.

While I was living with my father in his one square mile hometown, I attended church, town hall meetings, and other places with him. Being a proud father, he is extremely glad to show me off to people he does and does not know. Daddy proclaimed to them that I came home to assist him. I thought to myself, "What does he mean, "I came home?" I am not from here. I was born in raised in a different place. A rumor quickly spread within the borders of that small town. "Mr. Reverend or Elder Farmer's daughter came home to take care of her father." I was met with smiles of acceptance or the warm greeting, "welcome home." I was never addressed by my name. My name didn't seem to matter there as I was called by my father's name. After a while, I just politely smiled. Although Daddy knew I wasn't physically from his hometown, he knew I was a part of him, and that town was the springboard of my legacy.

I was going to live with my dad for a moment. I was excited to get an opportunity that I always wanted. It was more like redeeming the time. When I wanted to live with my dad, it was not feasible at that time. Therefore, I missed a lot of information and wisdom from father to daughter. I felt that instead of assisting him, I would be given assistance, and I was. I would be receiving impartations of wisdom, knowledge, family history, as well as a "male's" point of view. I was not sure of the amount of time I would be with Daddy.

However, I was fluid and open to the move of God in this event and for the events that have occurred to bring me to this point. I would be remiss if I didn't share a funny story during my 2014 birthday visit with my father. I flew from Colorado to spend my birthday with my dad. He treated me like a princess buying me things and introducing me to his friends and the town's people. He brought me birthday cupcakes and prepared dinner. However, there was a twist of events. Daddy had prepared meat and greens and told me if I wanted something else, I would have to cook it, so I did. After dinner, Daddy came to me with an apron in his hand that I had given him some years ago. He said, "Do you remember this?" "You gave this to me. Would you mind washing the dishes?" "I didn't get the chance to acknowledge the apron." I said, "But Daddy, it's my birthday." Daddy gave me a certain look that a father would give to his little girl after questioning a chore assignment. I obliged and washed the dishes. On-the-other-hand, washing dishes is not Daddy's greatest desire, and I know that. I find it hilarious now. During my childhood years, he told me to wash the dishes, and I was upset. I told him that "when I grow up, I won't make my children wash dishes, that I would have a dishwasher." Daddy's reply was, "We'll see when you have children…" I got married and had children, and they will have to tell you whether or not if they had to wash dishes.

It's not a secret that children seek the approval of their father/mother, present or absent. The lack of a father/mother leaves an empty space the child will try to fill by any means necessary. We are created to be fulfilled. As my father's daughter, I was always looking for his approval for my

accomplishments and desired goals. If he said, "that's good, baby/honey."
His words of affirmation to me were soothing and encouraged me to do
more. If he said "no," "you can't do that," or "it will never work," etc. I
became unsettled and wanted to know why he said what he said; I also
wanted to know why he wouldn't think it would work for me… He would
then tell me "why" according to his experience or beliefs. If it didn't make
sense to me, I would then set out to prove that I could do the impossible. I
have to laugh at this point because I remember we would get into arguments
about our differences of opinion. Eventually, daddy would allow me to do
what I was bold enough to do. He would allow experience to be my teacher.
Daddy, as the subject matter expert, would say either, "I told you so," or
"You did what you said you would do." "I didn't think it would work, but it
did." I understood that Daddy was trying to protect me from harm. Although
I am an adult with adult children of my own, he still tries to take care of and
protect me. I accept this as something that will never change as long as he
lives.

As I lived with Daddy, I got to see him in a new light. He respects that I am
an adult. However, there are a few times he slips in an opportunity to treat
me as his baby girl again. I am grateful that he prepared a room for me
decorated with pink and lavender accessories with a princess lamp. He even
presented me with a chocolate candy bar with the words "Princess." Being a
parent to adult children, I understand and don't blow up at him for my
independence. I feel comfortable with him, and I don't feel like I have to

prove myself. I can be myself. I can be Cynthia without reserve. Daddy can be himself without reserve.

We were happy to be living together again. We talked and enjoyed each other's company. We shared quality time talking about stuff like Bible topics and spirituality, family history, relationships, sports, politics, etc. One of the particular highlights was my father obtaining his long dream of owning a church to carry on his father's legacy. It was a privilege to assist him in the grand opening through cleaning, staging, catering, and ushering. To my surprise, he allowed me to teach Bible study with him. We also enjoyed laughing, going to church, shopping, health appointments, and some travel. "Bless the Lord," Daddy even gave me the talk." He even shared with me a father, brother, son, and male perspective about life and relationships. I waited over forty years for this! Better late than never.

After four months of interesting living with my dad, I wasn't surprised to see our likeness. I am a part of him. Receiving the blessing of learning from him and receiving the legacy to pass on to my children has been paramount. This has been one of the most beautiful times of impartation. I got to vote with my dad in our hometown for the first time. Together we enjoyed Veterans Day, Thanksgiving, Christmas, New Years' Day and saw the 2016 presidential results.

Coming home for me was coming back into myself. Coming home for me was being the individual that I knew I could be. It was the father, the brother, the son, the uncle, the friend I knew that was inside of me. Coming home for me was being the man that my mother reared me to be. Coming home to me meant being the family representative that needed me to take them to their destiny. Coming home to me meant being the whole person. It meant taking my life experiences and lessons to teach others. Coming home to me meant leading, influencing, and motivating people. It meant I'm moving on. Finally, coming home meant my parents seeing me as the person I was before they left or left this earth.

I felt healthy, sober, more armed, fit, and wise to help others conquer their struggles, demons, and wars. Every person faces some kind of fear whether or not they want to face it. You wonder if you will live up to the recognition you get or if you will fall back into the trauma of the war you just came out of. A person may fear rejection or if they regain a lot of parts of their lives. I was scared that maybe I had lost my desire to succeed or if I would become non-existent again.

Sometimes returning citizen has to return to their roots in order to grow. A tree needs its roots to grow. It doesn't just grow arbitrarily. Wherever those roots are that caused you to flourish is where you may need to return. Anything made of carbon, which is the main element of life, must return to its roots to feed and develop again. The first place I returned to, was my mother's house. She needed me, and I knew that she would accept me without judgment. I knew with her spiritual foundation; she understood the trials and tribulations more. Her arms were always opened to accept anyone needing assistance into the fold or household. After I felt more confident, I visited my father. I had outlived the purpose of why I was out there. I had lost interest and had outgrown my homelessness and addiction. I was tired of being tired and tired of the life I was living.

I was born to be a king in whatever arena I chose. Sometimes a king has to come off his throne to realize that he is a king. Sometimes he has to dwell around the folks that he is supposed to help rule over to remember what his purpose is and why he was chosen. Sometimes a king has to fall down to find out what makes him a king. Knowing you are a king is half the battle. Being king is another part of the battle. Doing it is the finished product of accepting whatever title you choose in life and doing it well.

Although a prince in my father's house, I was a "king in waiting." I was a king in developing and learning. Kings can meet with other kings to discuss better ways, better tactics, and a better understanding of how to rule kingdoms. It doesn't make a king less of a king to do so. For instance, a group of "alpha males" can get together to talk about ways to be a better alpha, a better person, or a better man. However, we are rightfully kings in our own right. The elder king accepts that he is among kings, but he is still given that mutual respect as being the senior king. His job is to dispense advice and knowledge. After the transition of the elder king, the next king in-line ascends to the throne.

The new king hopes to apply the knowledge and wisdom that he received from the previous elder king. The new king must constantly reflect on the teachable moments in life that prepared him for that moment in life that he may be wise and intelligent.

You can't do anything without a good foundation. Nothing can stand without a good foundation. You can't be who or what you plan to be without a good foundation. A tree doesn't stand and prosper without good roots. A house will not stand without a good foundation. Nothing in life stands without foundation.

<u>Enlightenment:</u>

Having an opportunity of redeeming time may be awesome. Sometimes it required returning to an earlier place such as a: hometown, organization, etc. It's going back to the basics to fill in the gaps that were not filled. It's getting answers and a better understanding of yourself and others. Redeeming the time can bring about necessary healing.

Home is not necessarily a physical abode. I learned home as being a state of mind that contains love, safety, and peace. Home can be with the people you love and who love you unconditionally. Home should be a place where you can be yourself without judgment. If you want to laugh hysterically out loud, you should be able to do that. At home, you don't have to justify who you are. If you want to let your hair down, pass gas, dream, build, etc., you should be able to do that.

Explain an area in your life where you would like to redeem the time. (Example: I always wanted to...)

____

____

____

____

____

____

What would that redeeming moment look like? (Example: I would apologize and start from now moving forward.)

____

____

____

____

____

____

____

If you are unable to redeem the time with someone, etc., how can you share your gift with others? (Example: I can mentor teenagers, women, men, etc.)

____

____

____

____

____

____

____

What is a note of gratitude that you can give that brought you to this point in your life? (I am thankful that I listen with my heart…)

____

____

____

____

____

____

____

Forgive and Rewrite the Story

"To forgive is to set a prisoner free and discover that the prisoner was you. ~Lewis B. Smedes

According to a John Hopkins Medicine Article on Healthy Aging, "People who hang on to grudges, however, are more likely to experience severe depression and post-traumatic stress disorder, as well as other health conditions."

Forgive others and ask for forgiveness – Forgive others for your benefit. Yes, you may have been really hurt, harmed, damaged, and scarred. Yes, it happened. You cannot change what has happened. However, you can change the outcome concerning you. We must forgive others so we can be free and get on with our lives. We need to forgive to be forgiven ourselves. We too have offended others in some way. In fact, there is a famous biblical scripture, Luke 6:37 (ERV) says, "…forgive others, and you will be forgiven. Forgive others, let it go, and move on with your life.

Unforgiveness is a prison that keeps begrudging people hostage. More than likely, the person(s) who may have wronged you is/are not thinking about how they offended or hurt you. It is highly likely that they are busy doing something else and have moved on with their life.

The information and recommendations contained in this section comes from tested authorities, The Bible, Medical studies (John Hopkins University), Louise Hay, author of "You Can Heal Your Life," and my personal experience.

In my personal experience I am reminded of an instance where I participated in a gossiping conversation with another person. Being the senior person in our living quarters at that time, I listened to my roommate concerns and observation of one of our other roommates. I thought her concerns were valid. I chimed in and began to share my opinions also. Little did I know, the roommate we were being judgmental and gossiping about was listening quietly in her room. As we continued to talk, our roommate walked out of her room into the living room area where I was sitting. She looked at me intently with tears and hurt in her eyes. She looked at me as if I had betrayed her and I did. I asked her to come and sit with me on the couch as I took responsibility for my actions and apologized to her. I was wrong and could not deny it. That was an embarrassing and awakening moment for me. The events that would follow was loss of credibility and having a talk with my supervisor. That moment would forever impress upon me the following reminders: Think before I speak; Refer gossipers to the person they want to discuss; Do not participate in gossiping; Remember, that what other people think of me is none of my business; Opinions are like behinds, almost everybody has one. Finally, it prepared me for walking in on being gossiped about and being lied on.

Here is my experience, from my point of view. I was working at a particular workplace after a change of leadership. What began to be a great working experience became a challenge for me. My decision to take a stand and voice my beliefs led to an imaginary target being placed on my back. My supervisor and peers appeared to have partnered with my senior leader to have me relocated to a different work assignment. I would walk-in on them gossiping about me or hear them talking about me before I came into a room. I asked my supervisor why I had to keep walking-in on them talking about me. I took mental notes. I was ordered to be the overseer for a retirement reception for my senior leader. I was also placed in charge of getting his retirement gift with $30 donated by my peers. I also was given a medium amount for the food, reception hall decorations and music. If things went wrong, my peers would not have to worry about being penalized. I was given a small budget to create a miracle with.

The first steps I took was to pray and see the event and tasks as my own. I forgave my offenders and found something nice to say about them. I pretended that my workplace was the best place to work. I obtained an external support group which helped me to keep my spirits up and endure my work environment. I wrote down all that needed to be done and began planning. Next, I had to get other people to help me pull off one of the greatest and memorable events. I went outside of my workplace and networked with other peers in the dining facility and part-time workers who were experienced culinary specialists who provided culinary supplies, chef attire and their services. I had a full staff. I had to get assistance from our audiovisual department which created a wonderful music playlist for the ceremony. I am thankful to my grandmother and parents for teaching me survival skills and how to manage a household and feed a large family with a minimal budget and minimal food. I began shopping six months early to get the drinks and other items on sale. I used coupons. I got the decorations from a dollar store. I went to a butcher and purchased other food items on sale and froze them. Regarding getting the retirement gift, I took the money and purchased items to make a wooden shellac clock with my senior leader's picture on it. On the day of the event, the presentation was spectacular, the food was delicious, and my senior leader loved his gift. It was at that time he said to me, "Chief, I realize that you are genuinely a great person." That compliment was worth its weight in gold. I felt that a big weight had been lifted from me. Other VIP's began calling requesting that I do the same ceremony for them. I referred them to the senior culinary specialist who was instrumental in making that event possible. I wrote letters of appreciations for my assistants. They were loyal and willing to help me. I could not have completed that event without them. They were my fairy godmothers and fairy godfathers.

Enlightenment:

If ever you find yourself in a situation that appears to be insurmountable, I encourage you to seek help. The help is available in different forms to include counseling, spiritual, emotional support, etc. Forgive your offenders and begin moving forward. Forgiveness is for YOUR benefit! It helps to keep you free and moving forward towards your goals. Forgiving has healing benefits. Forgive so you can be forgiven (Luke 6:37).

Action Steps Towards Forgiving:

1. Think of one person, dead or alive, who offended you.
2. Write their name on a sheet of lined paper.
3. Write a letter to your offender about the offense and how you feel/felt about it.

4. Read the letter in front of a mirror (audibly). How do you feel? This is where I recommend applying Louise Hay, Mirror Exercises contained in her book, "You Can Heal Your Life." I found it personally, emotionally, and spiritually helpful.

5. Rewrite the story and include the nice things about the person and yourself. It should also contain goodness, love, and abundance.

6. Read your new story audibly in front of the mirror.

7. Begin moving forward by taking one moment/day at a time.

Three Types of Men

In a woman's lifetime, she usually meets three types of men. They are called the Alpha, Bravo, and Charlie type men/personalities.

Alpha

The Alpha guy is mostly feared by the Bravo and Charlie guys. Unlike the Bravo and the Charlie men, especially the Charlie man, he has to beat his chest and always say, "Talk to me like a man. I'm the man." He has to keep reminding himself and the woman that listens to him that, "He's a man." Those are his favorite words or "F" this and "F" that. So, when the Alpha man comes on the scene, a true Alpha, he is very self-supporting. He has either a middle class or white-collar job.

The important thing is not just the job. It's the way he carries himself. He probably has experienced the highs and lows in life. He doesn't always have to be soft-spoken. He's more confident about himself and his situation. You won't hear him say, "I'm the man," because it's self-evident. He usually gives the woman "the look" or way of himself where she feels safe. My best friend, my wife, gave me the term *"little girl safe."* I never thought of it that way, but that's what it is. When you are a little girl, and you are with your daddy, big brother, or somebody you feel really confident or secure with. She calls it *"little girl safe,"* and I tend to agree with that.

He usually bumps heads with the strong female/woman, but after a few engagements like that, she usually gives him the nod of letting him "run the course, run the show." It's because she's gotten so strong dealing with the Bravo and Charlie guys; sometimes, it's hard for her to give way to the Alpha guy. However, she learns to respect him and let him do what he can. She doesn't necessarily fall behind him. She falls to the side. She gives him advice, and he respects her, so he will listen to her advice, and usually 80 to 90 percent of the time, he may follow that advice. When a decision absolutely, positively must be made, and she respects him as the Alpha male, she will let him make the decision. That's a position that he has to earn, and she has to earn his respect by allowing him to run the show. It usually takes a moment. With women constantly running into the Charlie and Bravo guys, they usually become stronger and stronger. In the end, sometimes it takes them a while to respect the Alpha guy but, if he carries himself well, like the true Alpha that he is, he earns their respect immediately.

1. What if there is a big Charlie male and a small-statured Alpha male?

Small in stature means either big in heart or big in brains. Sometimes, the Alpha man can use the Charlie man or the Bravo man's large stature against him, making him feel inferior anyhow. I speak from experience because I at one time was small in stature, but I was considered a nerd. I had guys like that (Bravo/Charlie) doing my bidding, doing my work. As the old saying goes, "It's not the size of the dog, it's the size of the heart of the dog that's in the fight. As we all may know, some of the most powerful men in the world have been small in stature but large in thinking, large in maneuvering, and large in commanding.

Some guys who are large in stature are put to the test to lead and don't know how to lead. They had been intimidating people with their size. As you spiritual folks do know, David did defeat Goliath. Sometimes large stature guys are making up for a lot of insecurities in other areas.

2. Examples: During my addiction stage, a lot of guys were intimidating in size. Once I realized that all they had was size, I could have them do my bidding because I did all of their business paperwork or all of their ready thinking. When they found out that they couldn't fight or intimidate their way through things, then their insecurities showed a lot.

3. When I was in college, once I showed guys that were bigger than me that I had just as much heart or more on the playing field of football, etc. I even earned more respect because they knew, once in the classroom where the playing field can sometimes turn to the advantage of a thinker. It's not who can lift the chair, but who can sit in the chair and do the thinking. We always knew that Einstein wasn't a real big man in the world but one of the smartest men in the world during his era.

If you think about some of the greatest men in the world, they were small in stature. Some of them include Einstein, Galileo, and Newton. George Washington Carver was small in stature and one of the greatest inventors in a lifetime. As I said, it's not the size. It's the size of the brain and the size of the heart of the man which decides to take on Herculean tasks in life. It's said that George Washington Carver was castrated. It's not the size of the penis or what a man can do with the penis. We have to remember; his penis may have been damaged or castrated. However, his brain wasn't. We are still using his inventions today. He gave away many of his inventions and patents.

Bravo

The Bravo-type men usually come on the scene, and sometimes, unfortunately, he's that real pretty guy. Women are instantaneously drawn to him. He's usually a "Momma's boy that has been taken care of by Momma or some woman because of his looks. He usually has a pretty decent job, but he swoons the women with soft words and that nice pretty smile and the charm that goes with all of that, and usually, the woman ends up taking care of him more so than the Charlie guy.

Charlie

The Charlie type personality man is usually the one that is holding himself, trying to act like he's a thug/gangster and all that type of non-bravado type "b.s." He either holds a part-time or low-level full-time job. He usually tries to intimidate women more or thug them. He tries to make them think that he's built like that. Especially with no other men around, he tries to make the women think that he's "the shit," as they say.

Queen, Princess, and The Mistress

Are you a queen (wife) or a princess? Are you a woman or a girl? Are you the mistress?

Queen - Cambridge dictionary says a queen is "a woman who rules a country

because she has been born into a royal family or a woman who is married to a king." MacMillian dictionary defines a queen as a woman with skill.

Wife - The woman with whom you are willing to spend the rest of your life with. The woman whom you don't want someone else to take her away from you; the woman that you find the most beautiful in this world, the woman who understands, makes your life complete and worth living till the end of it with her, the woman who is gonna be your soccer team's mother, and the woman that you are willing to give up your life for (https://www.urbandictionary.com/).

Princess - According to dictionary.com, a princess is a non-reigning female member of a royal family. The princess is also a daughter, granddaughter, daughter-in-law of a monarch. In my opinion, a princess is a glorified term for a girl.

Woman – An adult female.

Girl - is an immature female. She is also defined as a female child under age 18.

Mistress - (noun): woman having a sexual relationship with a married man; a woman in control of a situation; woman in charge of house and servants. (https://www.macmillandictionary.com/us/dictionary/american/mistress)

The Queen/Wife/Woman comes with her own stuff. She brings what she already has and combines it with her king/husband/man. She is resourceful and a helpmate to him. She can still be herself unapologetically while being his whisper during the storms of life. She is his best friend. She is not a nag. Although there are other beautiful women he may see, his thoughts are with his queen. Her demeanor causes her king to want to come home to be by her side. He wants to love and do more for her. A king recognizes a queen.

The Princess/Girl depends on her king/father to make provisions for her. In fact, she feels entitled and expects him to protect and provide for her as his princess/daughter. She does not have to work to get her needs, and some of her wants met. All she has to do is ask her father for what she needs or desires. If she knows how to ask her father for something, she may receive more.

The princess may praise the king on his strength or abilities, etc. Her appreciation and acknowledgment of his position and provision often translate to respect in his ears. Often, her father is more apt to give his princess more than what she originally requested, thereby spoiling her.

Some women have the princess/girl mentality when meeting a man. They are looking for men to take care of them. They ask the question, what can he do for me? Can he pay my bills and get my hair and nails done? Can he buy me a house or a car?

There is a princess or little girl in most women. We want to feel *"little girl safe"* while being treated like a queen. Little girls want to feel safe and want their daddy to make things better for them. However, since the king is in control, he can command his daughter to obey him. If she doesn't want to obey or get what she wants, she may pout, cry and throw a tantrum, hoping to turn her father's heart towards her and oblige. The princess does not really have a voice unless the king gives in.

We should be reminded that nothing is free. In order to receive, we must give something in exchange for a service rendered. Ladies, if you are looking for a Sugar Daddy, so to speak, to give you the desires of your heart, then you should be prepared to honor his requests. His requests may be uncomfortable for you. On the other hand, if you want to continue in the luxury lifestyle he provides, prepare to "put out."

We often see the **Mistress** as a homewrecking narcissistic woman with low self-esteem who desires attention, intimacy, and gifts from an unavailable or married man. Although, this may be true. A mistress is not just a woman. Shall we look at different shadows and types of mistresses? The mistress may be certain family members, churches, clergy, careers, etc. Entanglements with mistresses can wreak havoc in marriages and families.

Due to personal experience and as a witness, I choose to highlight a *type* of church and a *type* of parent.

Church - Some clergy use scripture and manipulation to encourage parishioners to spend much of their time attending services and giving money and services (legal, handyman, etc.) to them personally and their church or ministry to the detriment of the parishioners. They tell the members that attending every time the doors are opened and giving to their own hurt are sure ways to heaven.

A married woman whose spouse does not attend church with her. Her spouse may be an unbeliever or may attend a separate church/organization. The wife may enjoy her church and want her family to be a part of this amazing phenom. She prays for her spouse and children that they would somehow see the light and join her in the church towards the heavenly blessings and heavenly home. If her spouse or children does not submit, they are deemed as being unequally yoked. Instead of drawing her family to "Christ" or "Higher Power," they seem to pull away and get further away from her. The family relationship becomes strained and may end in separation or divorce.

I'm reminded of a sermon, "A Man Does Not Need Love" by the late Dr. Myles Munroe, Sr. I respect his response to a married woman parishioner who often attended church without her husband. There was a woman who attended his church, and her husband never attended with her. One day during a prayer meeting, Dr. Munroe asked the woman, "Where is your husband?" She replied that he was home and didn't believe in church. Dr. Myles proceeded to write an apology letter to her husband for keeping her away from him. Additionally, he wrote that he was sending her home because he (the husband) is her (the wife) priority. After signing the letter, he instructed her to leave bible study right away and go home to give her husband the letter. The following Sunday, her husband attended church with her. He met Dr. Munroe and expressed his appreciation for what Dr. Myles Monroe had done. Soon afterward, her husband kept attending, became a believer in the Lord, and joined the church. His wife was filled with joy. Dr. Myles showed her husband *respect* and did what some clergy will not do. He understood the order of marriage and the family. He wanted to help restore the family order, which led to the couple attending church together and bonding closer.

Parents - There are parents who sacrifice and work hard to provide for their children with the intention of their children taking care of them or becoming the person their parents want them to become (doctor, lawyer, athlete, preacher, etc.). These parents may not realize or care that they are clipping their children's wings by putting guilt on their children. They sometimes want to mold their children into what they want instead of their giftings or thing(s) that make them happy. Ask yourself these questions: Have you noticed your child getting upset when you tell them what they are going to become? Does your child participate in other events to avoid you? Did they move away for reasons you disapprove of? Do you know what interests them? Making your children responsible for your happiness is not their responsibility. Your happiness is your responsibility.

In conclusion, princesses attract princes, girls attract boys, women attract men, queens attract kings, and mistresses attract emptiness (the insecure, unfulfilled, married, or a person in a committed relationship).

The True Leader

"There are Four Senses: Street sense, School sense, Common sense and the sense to know which one to use at the appropriate time." Charles Brooks, Sr.

A lot of these wordings and theories come from practice over a long period of time. People who have put into play certain phrases, certain motivational phrases, certain driving phrases. One phrase is, "teamwork makes the dream work." Success without effort is calling for failure. Those sayings come from people who have tried or have been a part of the success of things/organizations or the failure of things/organizations.

You have to find a reason to make people believe in you or what you can do. If you haven't been successful or haven't completed anything yourself, how can you make others believe in you? How can you motivate anybody else? You don't even believe yourself? You have doubts yourself. You need to be part cheerleader and wear a lot of hats.

First, you got to believe in making somebody believe in you. It reminds me of that old "Car Wash" movie song where "Daddy Rich," a reverend, was played by Richard Pryor with the Pointer Sisters as the "Wilson Sisters." First, you have to believe. They sang the song, "You got to believe in something."

You have to believe in something to get something or to feel

(you know).

Reverend Ike and all great leaders had to get people to believe. Dr. Martin Luther King, Jr. had to get people to believe that he had a dream. The dream is what everybody is supposed to dream. Especially black people as a whole that they would be able to ride the same bus, sit at the same counter with the whites. So, you have to find a dream or idea that people can believe in or feel is possible. Just like R. Kelly sang in his song, "I Believe I Can Fly," and there you go. If you can see it, you can dream it.

The first part of solving a problem is you got to see it. You have to first see yourself in it. Why do you think you have these posters hanging over top of the bedroom door? The big house, the Rolls Royce, this, that, trip, and stuff. You got to believe. (*Cynthia)* You're always telling me, "…see it." People always say, "don't talk about it, be about it." It's got to feel possible. Just like my nephew told me, "I'm hard-headed." Yeah, I'm hard-headed, knowing that I can be successful. I tell folks, whatever energies I put in negative behavior and negative imagery, I have to put that same energy into successful behavior and successful imagery.

There are many distractions along the road, many hurdles, and obstacles. If I am head-strong and hard-headed, knowing that something better is down the road. Sometimes, the best motivator is you. You never know what people really think about. The people you think are with you, cheerleaders down the road, are some of your major distractions because they're scared that you will obtain more success than them.

Some of the people you think are your distractors are really motivators. I tell people all the time, "if you ain't trying to do nothing, you ain't got no haters." Haters motivate you. Haters make you levitate. You know, "if you aint got no haters," you aren't trying to do anything. It doesn't really have to be haters; it can be doubters. Sometimes we use the term haters, but they're doubters.

Doubters, just like people who doubted that I could overcome the obstacles that I placed myself in. The more doubters I get, the more I want to accomplish. They may not be haters, just doubters. Sometimes they can make you doubt yourself. Once you overcome one thing, now you're at the feeling. When you're already torn up somewhere else in life, whether it's financial, emotional, you start bringing yourself down in all areas because you can't get past that period.

When someone is broken in another area, it's sometimes hard to cheer them up to make them know they can succeed. You have to think about what they are succeeding in or what they are good at. That's what you do on your job. That's what I do in life. Alright, okay, so you don't have a Rolls Royce, but you have a bicycle. You're still better off than those that are walking. Okay, you don't have a six-bedroom home, but you have an apartment. It's better than living on the street. It's better than looking up and seeing the sky at night. At least you see a ceiling. Let's talk about what you do have. Just like it has been asked, "If money was no object, what would be your dream?"

These are the steps to your dream. This is how you go about getting to your dream. First, you have to believe. You have to see yourself with it. The more I thought about my *65th birthday party celebration*, it got me to thinking about a lot of things. People that I looked at in a certain way for strength were looking at me for strength. Although my nephew used a "**t**" in fai**t**h for talkative, which I am, I also use that "**t**" for **t**enacity, knowing that I'm going to keep hitting it.

I'm going to keep taking big rocks and making them into small rocks that I can carry or taking those big rocks and make a smooth road. The only time you can make big rocks smooth is you got to keep hitting at it. You got to keep hitting at it. You got to keep hitting at it. Some folks, after two or three hits at the big rock and the big rock, don't crumble or move or anything; they lose interest or faith. They want somebody else to do it for them and then want to enjoy the ride or the hard work of that individual who did that.

In boot camp, the leaders kept telling us to "move that boulder." The object was to move the boulder. Of course, a bunch of macho men will always try to think about using strength and pushing, and this yielded little or no tangible result. I guess the concept was to get everyone pushing together, just like we use the concept of working as a team. I was reared by an individual that believed in working smarter, not harder. I was in some regards, as people would say, "lazy." I believe in working my mind than my back. My father always says, "Your mind lasts longer than your back."

Sometimes people get caught up with their macho emotions trying to see who is the strongest. Men will sometimes have "pissing contests," of who can piss the hardest and the longest and all of that… In the beginning, we started pushing this rock. I said, "Oh, I said there is a better way." That's how a man came up with the wheel and other inventions figuring there is another way to get this mission accomplished. I saw like a railroad tire type thing. There is a better way. There's got to be a better way and still get what you need accomplished.

Look around your environment. That means whether it's your environment of people, your environment of places, your environment. There is something always around your environment that can help you get your mission accomplished because this is not the first time that it may have been asked of you or asked of somebody to do something, and we don't use the resources that are among us because we are in selfish-mode or ego-mode. So, we don't pay attention to the things around us. That's even in life. The wheel is already invented.

The only thing they have done with the wheel for years and years has made the wheel smoother, more comfortable, or usable. Do you notice that they haven't come up with a square wheel or rectangle wheel? So, the wheel is already there and has already been invented. So, you learn to use that wheel that's around you to your best advantage. So, after all that sweating and people passing out from exhaustion, I look around, and I see a railroad plank. Since I got individuals around me, that believe in being really strong, and you know, because the railroad plank is really heavy. Those things are thick and well preserved. They are built real sturdy. Remember, sometimes the thing that's built really well isn't built really tall. How could a normal man move it? Sometimes it's ingenuity. I took the guys that liked lifting and always figured they wanted to use muscle, you know, brawn over brains. I had them lift it up, so they felt part of the team. They felt good lifting up something heavy, and you know flexing.

Afterward, I got one of the guys to move another rock next to the big rock. I got those guys that were good at measurements and leverage and everything. The guys that weren't comfortable with themselves, I had them clear out a little path between the two rocks. Everybody pitching in felt like they were part of a team. We stuck the railroad plank between the two rocks, and so, even the guys that weren't as strong I had them push the big rock. At the same time, I had the stronger guys pull down on the plank. It was leverage. The doubters began to see.

I painted a picture of how we could make this work. Of course, the doubters were talking about the plank breaking. I had to remind them this plank has between fifty to hundreds of tons of steel riding across that thing. It has to be strong enough or else, they wouldn't use it. They thought like you thought, "it's too short." How tall does it have to be? The planks are going to be used for a brief moment by a train. The train's speed going across it won't be on it for long, only on departing and arriving. The weight is equally distributed. So, when the big rock didn't move at first, then you start getting your doubters. "Man, you don't know what you're talking about. You're just all mouth." I said, let's readjust this plank again. Get it down deeper, closer to the bottom of the big rock. "Ah man, you always…" I said, "Alright." So, I grabbed the one that was giving the most opposition. I said, "Yo, come here, man." "What do you think?" I got him involved. I really wasn't listening to him but, I got him involved. I got him to help motivate the other doubters.

Sometimes you have to get the leaders of the doubters more involved or give them a position you really didn't want to. Sometimes they doubt because you were placed in charge, and they weren't put in charge. So, you give them an important role, but you still supervise. Once you give the doubter a role and he's motivated, it takes the focus off you and puts it on him. In the meanwhile, he's your main cheerleader but, he's cheering for himself. So, it's all the forces working the same way. Everyone is pushing the cart the same way.

The leader is a great organizer, a great read of people and their strength. As we say, "He knows how to eliminate certain opposition." He looks at other people to see the one who is his major opposition and gives him an important role. If he knows that someone is just as strong as he is, he knows that he may have a weakness in a certain area, he may give him that role. A role for him to shine, and they form a bond.

I gave the doubter a role that made him feel like he was in charge. Sometimes you can pick a person to lead and find out they are not a leader. They are a good follower, or they may have to be taught to lead. In those circumstances, you also learn about people, and you learn about yourself. If you can't delegate and want to do everything yourself, then you're not a leader of people. You're not even a leader. You're selfish.

Sometimes you're going to run into strong personalities, and if you feel that you don't want to work with them because they are too strong, then you're not a good evaluator of people. Sometimes you need to take that strength and use it to your advantage to get other hard-headed or determined people to follow you. It's just like you may be in charge.

It's like an officer, he may have the rank, but the highest-ranking NCO (Non-Commissioned Officer) has the trust of the men. So, if you're the leader, you're the officer coming to order people around or disrespecting the NCO, but when you really need a mission accomplished, if the NCO says, "Let's make him look bad;" they'll make him look bad because the men trust the NCO. They have been in situations where they trusted him. Trust make leaders.

Even when we had individuals come on the job and because they want the (leader) position, that doesn't mean they are a leader. I was famous for telling folks that I didn't have confidence in or I didn't trust them; I let them know, "you are not my leader." You know, you may be the one in charge, but you're not my leader. They have to earn that because, not every man believes that they are a leader. They just weren't given the opportunity. Sometimes the opportunity is forced upon them. The opportunity given to some people they placed in charge, sometimes panicked and realized that they were not the leader they thought they were.

Sometimes leaders come out of situations and problems. Leaders are those a group of people feel can lead them out a problem, out of a situation or hazard. That's how leaders are sometime come about.

In regard to the boulder, once I got my main *opposition* to play into the role or be about assisting me. Instead of constantly putting up with opposition why it wouldn't work, I got him to help, you know, he became fully involved.

We took the railroad log, put it between the little rock and the big rock to act as a leverage. I had people pushing the big rock at the same time we were pulling down on the railroad log. Once we were able to get some movement from the big rock and would pull down on the railroad log, we picked the big rock up. It had settled in the ground so deep that it was hard to push it because it had built itself a hole.

Once we got the big rock to get a little bit up in the air, it was easy, and with the forces of the push, we got it to get on a little roll, and once it got to rolling, we just got out of the way and let gravity and the help get it going. We let it stop on its own. Luckily and fortunately, it had an area where the ground leveled off, and it stopped on its own. The idea was to see if we could work as a team or a unit to move the rock. We were told that the rock had not really been moved before. It might have been moved an inch or maybe a foot but because it was so settled in its spot, a lot of the organizations, and men gave up because no one thought to use a leverage. Using a leverage set a precedent of finding the right person with the right mindset and it took a little bit of "moxie" as they say, which determined, we could move that thing.

I was a PFC/E2 in the Army boot camp at that time. That experience bonded me with a lot of guys that were in the squad. It let them know that I was a thinker. Although I was also very vocal about my opposition to being in the military, being a thinker, caused guys to listen to me. It took some of the followers away from the guy that was a nonbeliever because, I had shown the guys that we could move the boulder. Although, I wasn't all that big and strong like Hercules, I always told them, I was a thinker. They tend to believe in guys who were like me, thinkers. They started feeling good about themselves, knowing that they didn't have to be six-foot, so-and-so with muscles rippling everywhere. They learned that they could be who they were and continue being a thinker. I was able to earn trust from a lot of individuals that would have taken me a lot longer *to earn.*

The Sergeant came running up to the squad asking, "How did we move it?" The people kind of suggested that I was the instrument of change. First of all, he couldn't believe it, and second, he was mad because it had been moved a lot further than maybe he wanted or expected, and third, he realized that the type of individual he thought that might one or two of the real big guys would be the instrument of change. When he saw it was someone like me, small in stature, big mouth, who spoke-up, wasn't intimidated by him, and someone without the military bearing that he was hoping to get.

In many ways the sergeant was intimidated. I knew that our time in the military was going to be tested on many occasions. The Sergeant knew that he had to be sure of his facts or information that he would relay to me because he knew I was going to challenge him.

The Rescue

Women who have been hurt or in hurting relationships may look to be rescued. They may be looking for that father/daddy persona to help them feel "little girl safe" and make it all better.

Once the needy girl-woman experience a man who may give her a gift or maybe buy her a drink or pay for her meal or ask her to dance, she may feel a sense of relief or hope. She may think to herself, "wow, this guy may be the one to take care of me." It may not matter to her if he is in a relationship or that he is on a date with another woman.

She could misinterpret his kindness as a flirt or desire to be with her. She may see this as a hunting opportunity. She may think, "maybe I can take him from the woman he's with. Certainly, I can be a better woman to him than she is, and he'll take care of me. That is such a misnomer. There are nice men who are just showing kindness with no-strings-attached.

The reality is we attract to ourselves people who are just like us. Sometimes, we may not like who we attract. If that is the case, we must then look inside ourselves. We must look in the mirror. The change must first begin with us. Trying to so call, "steal a person from another is only inviting the same situation to happen to the initiator. We are our own rescue. We are responsible for our own rescue. We can begin by working on self-development in needed areas.

There are various areas of counseling available to assist us in being the better version of ourselves. I believe that making needed changes within ourselves by being the change we want to see will attract our heart's desire. "Like attracts like." We must first love ourselves.

The Champion Season

"No man is an enemy. No man is a friend. Every man is a teacher." Unknown

The champion season to me is the mentality that men and women must take. For the most part, men have an idea how to work that, how to do that. Women for the most part, haven't gained that mentality yet because they… Men have big egos. Don't get me wrong, but sometimes, we know how to shut the ego down or put it aside. What I mean by that is, two men can be on the same team, can't stand each other, you know, and it comes almost to hate. A strong coach can recognize that those two individuals have the most skills, but they are not working together as a team. So, he usually sits both of them down in a room. One *player* usually has the most hate but is the better blocker. He's the blocker of men, and blocker of ideas and can single focus. The other one usually has great skill at maneuvering people, things, and obstacles. The coach explains to the one that is really strong and says, "look, I need you to put aside your hatred or dislike or whatever term you use for this man right here." He will usually have them in a room together and say, "for us to reach that championship, for us to reach our primary goal, which is to win the championship, so we can get this money, or get this prestige, I need for you whether it's temporary or permanent to remove your problem with this man." To the man that has less skill but really good at maneuvering, he will say, "I need you to put away your hatred, your dislike, or whatever term you use, with this man to score this touchdown.

If ya'll can't do that, we may as well pack it in and say that we're not going to try to win the championship." So, what ya'll want to do, because, all eyes on the team are watching ya'll? Can ya'll put away your personal problems with each other so we can score this touchdown, so we can win the championship, so that we can get the trophy, so that we can get the money, so you can do whatever your lifestyle is, so that you can do it on a grander scale? What do you want to do?

Most men, not all, but most men will temporarily put those feelings aside to do that. Some of them soon learned to like, love, or appreciate each other, i.e., "Remember the Titans." In Remember the Titans, there was a lot of racial prejudice and stereotype. But men can *put aside their differences*. Whereas women for the most part, won't do that. They can, but they won't because they keep letting their little personal pride, ego, jealousy, and envy keep them from achieving the success that they can. Some women will say, I'm not doing anything for that "B" "the hell with that "B" and won't do it." Women organizations and teams that can get that "men mentality" usually are the most successful organization because women may not be as strong as men physically, but they are just as cunning and ruthless, and have so many skills. What men have over them is, they will not only say it they will do it. Women will say it, but sometimes at the last minute will change their mind and won't do it. Until women stick with the same mindset, they will not achieve much success as they possibly can. It's no way that women are not supposed to be in charge of a majority of things on this planet because it's usually more of them. They think when men are asleep, but they don't have that "stick-to-it-ness" because they get jealous over how other women dress, talk, or this and that, and stay with that. Men will compliment another man's suit, pair of shoes, or his smoothness. Women will say, "Yeah, look at that dress, look at those shoes or look at that walk." They find something to nitpick or hate-on. They will get mad because someone may be attracting more of the opposite sex than they are. She won't block for her and do what's required because she didn't get that man or get the attention of that man.

One of the greatest successful women's college sports teams is the University of Connecticut (UConn), Women Huskies, which I have watched for many years. They won all thirty-three games (33-0). Another year, they won thirty-two games and lost one (32-1). They have won more than two college basketball championships. Their coach, Coach Gino, one of the major things he teach them is using, "the man's concept of championship," which is to, put away pettiness, jealousy, and envy. UConn, has a reputation for winning. If they can't put away those issues, then they don't want them. It's like that movie that says, you have to "think like a man even if you act like a woman."

Many women organizations have not succeeded because they don't know how to think like men in achieving certain things. They get sidetracked, they get hoodwinked. Women that are very successful in life may get called names by men because some men don't like real competitive women unless they themselves are strong enough. But they really respect her especially if she does it the right way. In most men eyes, the way a woman does it the wrong way, is when she sleeps her way up the ladder or is dishonest. If she's been in an abusive relationship and it carried her to the top, then maybe that's her reward. But if she didn't put in the hard work, she's not going to be respected. Women who come from male dominate industries and have "worked their way up and not slept their way up" are usually well respected because they know what it takes to build a champion season.

Self-Sabotage

Have you ever prayed and asked God or someone for something, and the answer came quicker than you imagined? You then decided and said to yourself, "this came too fast," or "it's too good to be true?" Maybe you said, "let me table this for a while, or put it on layaway." Have you ever said, "I'll give it some time, and if the answer is still there, then it's meant to be?" I call these thoughts and behaviors self-sabotage.

There are some things that will come to us very quickly because we need them right now to continue our journey. In living our purpose, some things will manifest quicker, and others may appear to take longer to show up. It is important to be mindful not to sabotage ourselves or the gift that we asked for. Remember, everything has a shelf life, even if it is on layaway. There is a window of opportunity for us to work within. Self-sabotage will cause you to miss an opportunity that may never come again.

I remember my mother keeping the good/fine dishes in the china cabinet. They only were used on special occasions. They sat there collecting dust until the holidays came around. Have you ever wanted to go on a trip or do something you found exciting and put it off for later? Maybe you spent the money and missed those opportunities? Here's a little secret, we cannot take anything with us. Everything that we get on this earth pertains to this earth and will remain on this earth. "The earth is the Lords and everything in it, the world, and all who live in it (Psalms 24:1)." After we die, we will take nothing with us. The only thing that is going to be leaving is our spirit from our body. Even our bodies will stay here and return to the earth to replenish it.

Enlightenment:

What we do not use, we lose. We are always living in the present moment of now. Tomorrow never comes. Doubt and procrastination lead to lack, poverty, and missed opportunities.

Your Story

What opportunity did you have that you should have taken and did not? (Example: I was granted a scholarship and did not use it before the deadline, etc.)

____

____

____

____

____

Why did you procrastinate? (Example: I didn't think I was good enough, etc.)

____

____

____

____

____

____

____

How can you apply what you have learned to a current opportunity today? (Example: I called and spoke with a career counselor to assist me with enrollment, etc.)

____

____

____

____

How do you feel by taking the first step towards your opportunity/goal? (I am thankful that I listened with my heart, took action anyway although, I was afraid, etc.)

The Chang-a-lang

The "chang-a-lang" is the sound I hear or the sound I cause people to hear. When I was working in the shelter and some of the guys/residents who worked different jobs would come and talk "crap," a load of stuff to me. They would have a pocket full of money and walk past my desk and say, "yeah, Mr. Brooks, how do you like this "lettuce (money)?" I would say, "That's nice," and I would be hungry and broke, barely having lunch money, or I didn't have lunch money.

They said, "Yeah," and would constantly throw the fact they had money in my face. I said, "Yeah, I got something better than lettuce." They said, "What's that?" I would dig in my pocket and shake my house keys at them. I said, "chang-a-lang, chang-a-lang. They asked, "What's that?" I said keys to my own place. I'm not living here in a shelter with 400 men. As I remembered and went on in life, I would give housing presentations every Wednesday when I started working with "Pathway to Housing" and even "Easter Seals."

I used to talk to individuals, mostly veterans talking to them about gaining their own apartment, their own house, or their own place. Whatever it was, condominium, house, townhouse, it didn't matter. I used to explain to them that the greatest sound I have, and they should have, is the "chang-a-lang." They would say, "chang-a-lang?" "What the hell are you talking about, sir?" I said you have gotten paid from a job, dug in your pockets, and pulled out handfuls of dollar bills, but you didn't have the "chang-a-lang."

The "chang-a-lang" is a set of keys to your own place. You might have stayed in a motel, hotel, Holiday Inn, and they got cards, so you won't hear the chang-a-lang. But you know you have made a giant step in your life when you're able to shake house keys, some type of keys to your own place. That's the greatest sound in the world, especially if you have been homeless, especially if you have been living with somebody else on their turf and their rules, on whatever. It wasn't yours. The greatest sound to be honest, it's when you have that "chang-a-lang."

When you stick that key in your door and knowing that you can close the world out from beyond when you know it's yours that you are paying and working for it. That's the greatest sound, especially to me and to anybody who didn't have their own set of keys to their own place. There's no other better sound than the "chang-a-lang."

It's Not You; It's Me

Have you ever worked for a company or organization, and it seems just like they weren't following the rules, or they weren't doing things right, and you got frustrated? What do you do? Well, I think a good answer to that, in my opinion, and from my experience, is that when things seem to be going wrong, the first thing is to check within yourself. I had to check within to see if there were any adjustments I needed to make.

For the most part, we begin with ourselves. We must take responsibility for our professional, personal, spiritual, and emotional development. After making the necessary changes, and it still seems like things are not working, then maybe it's time to go.

Sometimes we look at the company saying, "This person is doing something wrong," or "The boss is not listening," and start pointing the finger. You may be right. However, what that situation could be telling you is usually a telltale sign that it's time to move on. Your assignment may be coming to a close. There is something better for you ahead.

Although sometimes we may get nervous or get a little scared, preparations are necessary to move onto something else. We are always arriving somewhere. When you go to the boss and put in your two-week notice or whatever that looks like for you-you can honestly say it's not you; it's me. When where you are working no longer aligns with where you are going, then it's imperative to move forward.

It's important to move forward to continue to grow. If we are not growing, then we are dying. We were not put here on earth to be stagnant. We were put here to produce and to be a part of a solution. I like the saying, "If I can't be a part of the solution, then I won't be a part of the problem." If you feel that you are becoming a part of the problem and you are not a part of the solution, then that may be a telltale sign that you need to move forward. If you look at the people around you that are the troublemakers, maybe you can look at them as your motivators, elevators, and encouragers. It may be helpful to view them as nudging you towards your greater purpose. They are doing what they are supposed to be doing, and that's encouraging you to move forward. Maybe it's a part of their assignment to help you into a new season in your life.

Please be advised that during your transition, friends and family may walk away from you. On the other hand, it's okay. Keep moving. If you stop moving because people whom you loved separated from you, it's not going to serve you well. You will lose. In order to win, you must keep forging ahead.

Keep moving forward and upward. It won't always make sense to everybody. Some people will think that you are crazy. It's okay to be an original because everyone else is already taken. Love yourself. You are enough. You have everything you need inside of you to accomplish your goals. Keep moving. If you stop moving, you cannot be a help to those elevators and haters or to the people that are coming behind you. We were meant to blaze the trail. Make a difference and move on. We were meant to leave a legacy of love. Your love legacy is wrapped in the purpose that was given to you to fulfill while you are on this earth for your prescribed time. It's not you; it's me. Love you, be you, and do you. It's not you, it's me.

The Four Types of Dogs

His Story

There are four types of dogs: The House Dog, Porch Dog, Yard Dog, and Neighborhood Dog. The house dog is the dog that the owner can put in their arms and carry in their bag and treat it like a little child. Then there's the porch dog. He has a little more freedom than the house dog. He sits on the porch and barks at everybody that passes by. He gives the impression that he's a hell-raiser. Next is the yard dog. He patrols the yard and walks around with his chest out. He's got everybody thinking that he's the shit. Finally, you have the neighborhood dog. He walks with no collar. He walks around the yard dog, barks at him, and tells him to "shut the hell up." He walks up on the porch and tells the porch dog to get the hell out of the way.

This neighborhood dog then knocks on the door, and when the house dog begins barking and everything, he usually eats his ass or bites his ass. He lets the house dog know, "I run this."

As you get older, you find out the type of dog you are, and you learn your boundaries and restrictions. What type of dog are you? My mentality and thinking is the neighborhood dog. Because of my responsibilities to my wife and being a husband and everything, I'm a combination of all the dogs. I have to be in the house to protect my house. I have to be a little bit of a porch dog to watch who's coming near or around the porch. I have to know my yard to see which dogs come through the neighborhood that I may keep an eye on them. I'm a combination of all the dogs.

Your finances and thinking determine what type of dog you're going to be that day, week, or month, or whatever is happening in your life. If you are married or have some financial responsibility, your finances can't be like the neighborhood. You can't be treating everybody like everything is on you, you know.

You got everybody's back and so forth. You have to start being selective in a lot of things. You then got to be like a house dog in your finances and your protectiveness. You have to protect your house and maybe your porch. So, that's how you have to start narrowing your thinking on which type of dog you are in certain aspects. For example, a family man with children needs to be more of a house dog, porch dog, and yard dog. If he does not have that many responsibilities or any, he can be the neighborhood dog that got everybody's back.

In other aspects, he must have some neighborhood dog thinking to know what's happening in his neighborhood. He must know what to be on alert for or know who is doing what, so when he sees that person near the yard, near the door, or the porch. He'll know what to brace for. He will know how to prepare himself. You have to have some yard dog and neighborhood dog in your thinking. You have to know who else is a neighborhood dog and what he can do.

What neighborhood do you come from? That is the way you can best battle, think, and act. It's like that saying, "You have to know what your enemy and competitor knows," so you can be ready to deal with him. Sometimes you have to think like a house dog, so you know where everything is in the house. You have to know who you have to protect first, who is the most vulnerable, and who is the weakest link. You have to know where any weapons are or where your help is. This is where you must have a house dog mentality.

It's important to know how far the porch extends, or where the strongest and weakest parts of the porch are, and where you can hide, leap or attack from.

You have to know a lot about your porch. It's knowing your property, your property line, and all aspects of your yard. Know where the weak link in the fence is. Know where you can get out and attack from or where you have to pull back and stand your ground. That's the aspect of the yard dog.

A good neighborhood dog has to be all of those dogs mentioned above for him to be effective. If he was just a neighborhood dog, the yard dog could take them to a part of the yard where he doesn't have that advantage and do him in. A house dog can close the door and lock him in a room or something or where he can't get at anybody. Sometimes the house dog knows how to put the latch on.

The yard dog may know how to use his nose or paw to take the latch off or put it on. He knows part of the fence he can get out or in or where to jump from. This is why I say, the neighborhood dog would have to have been all the different dogs before, so he'll know how a neighborhood dog thinks, act or where his help comes from. This will allow him to brace or be able to "talk that talk" with him. He may say, "Yeah, I was hanging out with you but, this is my house. This is my yard, and you're not going to be peeing or crapping in my yard." This is my woman. Sometimes she comes into the yard, sits on the porch, or be in the house. That's how it is."

A Call to Response

The physical death/transition of loved ones is meant to bring awareness to ourselves. It is a call to respond. This awareness is that physical life will come to an end, and we don't always know when. The awareness is a reflection of who you are. What do you look like in your metaphorical mirror? With this given time, what are you doing? Are you putting it off until tomorrow what you can do today?

When a person dies, we often hear, "you can't take it with you." I challenge the statement that "you can't take it with you." "The earth is the Lord's and the fullness thereof (Psalm 24:1, KJV)." Although you cannot take the tangible things that belong to this earth and can only be used on this earth with you, you can however, take your potential, dreams, and ideas of inventions, etc. Dr. Myles Munroe, Sr. is noted for his reiteration that "the richest place on earth is the cemetery where a person's potential has died with them. They took songs that were never heard, paintings that were never painted and books that were never written, etc."

In my transparency, I would like to share my awareness with you. Between 2012 and 2014, I lost eight people that were dear to me. In 2015-2016 two of my dearest cousins transitioned. July of 2019, my late husband, Donald Brooks, and co-author of this book passed-away. In 2020 my family's senior matriarch, Aunt Winnie 107, and another cousin 92 gained their heavenly wings. They had a major impact on my life one way or another.

From these people, I was able to see what motivated them. I was able to witness some of their passions. I saw the current results in their life that stemmed from past events and habits. I listened to stories that they shared with me about their lives that either excited or angered them. I became a student. I asked questions and listened to their answers. I watched the joy on their faces when they talked about their accomplished goals of providing for their family through hard work and perseverance. I also witnessed the agony, anger, and grief on some of their faces as they shared the injustices they experienced. I listened to a couple of them complaining about the medical attention and assistance they were experiencing in their final days. They were frustrated with helplessness, fear, and the need to have others assist them. There was also noted fear of the concern of who would take care of loved ones in their stead. They were no longer in physical control of their coming and going. I heard one say that he was "not ready to give up his throne yet." He had created an empire and wanted more time. That was the day I saw a "great king," my late father-in-law and family patriarch cry. From the hospital bed, he continued to work. He fought off the surly bounds of death to no avail. During his transition, the room grew cold. He slipped away with family at his side. Soon afterward, the initial shock and screams of panic and grief-filled the room. "You can't leave us…" "Who's going to take care of us?" were the cries that filled the hospital corridor on August 16, 2013. It was also during that time, I learned that my very own dear mother suddenly became very ill. I left my late father-in-law's side to rush to my mother's side.

Upon arriving in DC, I saw that my mom's countenance was dim. She looked as if she had aged ten years from the previous month when I last visited her. My mother's make-up was to always appear strong in front of her children, family, friends, and co-workers. I guess I could say that would include everyone she was trying to be strong for. I was one of the few people she would let down her guards with. She could be vulnerable and trust that I would do everything I could to help her. During her illness, she began to grow weaker and became helpless as a little child. Our roles of positional authority were switching. I became her support and protector. She called out for me and looked for me, and expected me to be there for her. I had to ensure that procedures and proper handling for her care and effects were being carried out. If I was not traveling for training or work, I had to be there. I had to be. What I thought was one of the most painful and difficult times in my life became one of the greatest blessings I would ever experience in life.

Everything that I felt I was missing in my relationship with my mother came around full circle. I remember the warmth of love I felt from my mother as a toddler. However, somewhere around the age of eight, I felt like her love was being taken from me. Ma needed my help. Being a single parent, she had to work to make ends meet that did not always seem to come together. I felt that I had been robbed of her affection. I was assigned continuing responsibilities of "growing up."

I was becoming more independent due to extenuating circumstances. For thirty-seven years, I yearned for the love I thought I was missing. I was made to be the responsible one among my siblings. Everyone depended on me to do the right thing. I often thought, "why me." Even during my mother's illness and physical death, I felt the demanding pressure to take care of everything. The people I thought would be present and helpful could not handle my mother's illness and stayed away. Therefore, I had to drive seven hours twice a week between two states and Washington, DC, to care for my mother and take care of her business.

Having to make decisions for a dying loved-one was not easy. Where was the relief? When was the cavalry coming to rescue us? I was not volunteering for this. I could not see the answer during that perilous time. Why me? Why did it seem like I was in it by myself? It was as if I was that preteen and teenager child again who was assigned the major household responsibilities. I was responsible for ensuring the household chores were completed. I was also the caregiver of my siblings while my mother was absent from our home. Ma knew that I would carry out her wishes for the most part. She trusted me to ensure that things went well. In the final moments of visiting with my mom, the answer came. It was in the "goodbye" or the proverbial "see you later." I was enlightened that I was made for that moment. I began kissing Ma's head where her hair had begun to grow back. She returned the love by tenderly kissing my hands and hugging my arms. It was one of my greatest gift exchanges of love that brought back those longing, early-age loving feelings I received from my Mommy.

I felt my mother's love as I once knew it to be prior to age nine. I received the flashback of a picture I kept, of sitting on her lap as she put on my little sneaker shoes. I felt her protection and nurturing love once again. On-the-other hand, the roles were reversed. I was hovering over mother, giving her a kiss and gentle hug, telling her that I love her. It was like, I was the parent, and she was the child. That was one of the greatest love's I shared with my mother. The greatest blessing for me I shall always cherish was that irreplaceable moment.

A Footnote to My Wife

Donald Brooks

Out of nowhere, out of somewhere, you came into my life. I have been alone but surrounded by people. You came into my life unexpectedly seeking help but really giving help. You came into my life not really looking for someone to come into your life, to be a part of your life, until you got your life settled and focused. It showed that we were like wandering lights in a tunnel that came together to become one light. It was not by design which makes it even that much greater.

We went out to entertain each other and take our minds off our individual issues or problems. I had to clean out a little more clutter in my life, but maybe you had your own clutter. Once we scraped our plates clean, we could take on the offering of food for our bodies and our minds. We were able to focus on the meal at hand. We realized that we liked and could prepare some of the same foods. It doesn't mean so much the food that you eat, but the foods and nourishment of life. We realized that we had some of the same goals and purposes.

Once, you (Cynthia) reminded me that you were the marrying type. I had to make sure that I was ready for you completely. Not just for the physical and social aspect of it but for life itself. It shows that we were really destined for each other because we have moved at a great speed acquiring the things we wanted. Some people call it the "trappings of life," which is ok.

It's what any reasonable human being is trying to acquire, which is their success and goals.

We also have gained what life is truly about, which is the joining of another human being to share the good, bad, and indifferent; to accept the highs and lows of a relationship, to deal with the disappointments and the achievements of one another and to be there in time of need, grief and sorrow and also the happiness. So, my footnote to my wife, Mrs. Cynthia Prospers Brooks is, to say thank you. Hopefully, we can continue to grow and overcome any obstacles that come our way because we have overcome and achieved so many already in our lives. We remember that we love each other, respect each other, and care for each other. I think we can reach that level of happiness that we both have sought, whether we did it verbally, internally, and externally. I want to tell you thank you.

Acknowledgements

I want to extend a special thank you to my beautiful niece Sharde' D'Vohna for designing the front of our book cover and Elder's collage. I also want to thank my siblings, Starn, Joel, Sherricka, and Jeremiah for their encouragement. Thank you to my cousins Crystal, Joan, CJ, Ida, John C., and Sandra, family and deep friends Dr. Ella and Tina V. Thank you Pastors A. and G. Brunson for your encouragement and support.